Minority Politics
and Ideologies
in the United States

CHANDLER & SHARP PUBLICATIONS IN
POLITICAL SCIENCE

General Editor: Victor Jones

Minority Politics and Ideologies in the United States

Jane H. Bayes
California State University, Northridge

Chandler & Sharp Publishers
Novato, California

Library of Congress Cataloging in Publication Data

Bayes, Jane H., 1939–
    Minority politics and ideologies in the United States.

    Includes bibliographical references and index.
    1. Minorities—United States—Political activity.
2. Women in politics—United States.   3. United States—
Politics and government—1945–   I. Title.
E184.A1B28   1982   323.1'73   82-17698
ISBN 0-88316-551-1

Copyright © 1982 by Chandler & Sharp Publishers, Inc.
All rights reserved.
International Standard Book Number: O-88316-551-1
Library of Congress Catalog Card Number: 82-17698
Printed in the United States of America.

Book design by Joe Roter.
Edited by W. L. Parker.
Composition by Publications Services of Marin.

SECOND PRINTING, 1986

To Kyle, Joseph, and Stephen

Contents

Introduction	1
1. The Ideological Frameworks within Which Minorities Operate in the United States	3
The Liberal Tradition	3
The Lockean Liberal Framework	4
The Pragmatic Utilitarian Framework	5
The Marxist Position	6
The Inadequacy of Traditional Ideologies	7
Minorities and Ideological Change	8
2. The Significance of Minority Politics	11
The Position of the Subordinate	11
Negative-Power Tactics	13
Breaking-Out Tactics	14
Dependency-Creating Tactics	16
The Strategic Situation of Minority Groups	21
3. The Minority Politics of Black America	25
Separatist Movements	26
The Garvey Movement	28
The Nation of Islam: The Black Muslims	31
Integrationist Movements	34
The National Association for the Advancement of Colored People	35
The Union Movement and Black Workers	37
Direct Nonviolent Mass Action: Core, SCLC, and SNCC	38
The Theory of Nonviolence	39
The Birth of the Black Power Movement	45

The Lowndes County Freedom Organization	47
The Black Panthers	48
Black Studies—Pan-African Movements	53
The International Orientation of Black Politics during the 1970s	55
Ideological Assessments of Black Politics	56

4. The Minority Politics of Women — 65

A Brief History	66
The Pragmatic Feminist Position	69
Strategies for Pragmatic Feminists	71
Antifeminist Arguments	72
The Radical Feminist Perspective	73
Strategies for Radical Feminists	74
The Socialist Feminist Position	76
Strategies for Socialist Feminists	81

5. The Minority Politics of the Chicanos — 85

A Brief History	87
Problems in Counting Undocumented Immigrants	89
Political Organization among Chicanos Today	90
The Strategic Position of Chicanos	92
Pragmatic Organizing Techniques	94
The Chicano Cultural Movement	97
United States-Mexican Relations: Chicanos and Immigration in the 1980s	98
Public Opinion in the United States	100

6. Ideological Change and Minority Politics — 107

The Role of Ideology in the Process of Change	108
The Pragmatic View of Ideology and Change	108
Critiques of the Pragmatic Utilitarian View	109
The Marxist View of Ideology and Change	110
The Linguistic or Semiotic Model of Change	111
The Role of Theoretical Activity	113
Specific Ideological Contributions of Minority Politics	113
An Assessment of the Semiotic Model as Applied to Ideologies and Minorities	118

Index — 120

Preface

The study of minority politics cannot be separated from the study of ideologies in a society. Political minorities who do not control military or police violence, who do not control the economic resources, and who occupy lower status positions are left with ideologies and symbols as their primary political resource. For minorities, the use of violence or economic sanctions becomes effective primarily when the circumstances allow such tactics to have a symbolic message.

While the study and practice of minority politics is extremely important for those who would redistribute the wealth and power in society, minority politics may also offer important insights into the role of ideologies in the process of political and social change.

A central premise of this book is that certain ideologies function in a way that is analogous to a language; they have a certain independent life of their own. Just as a language cannot be understood without speech, political ideologies have meaning in relation to human interactions. As language transformations develop through speech, ideological innovations develop from changes in patterns of human interaction. Individuals through their speech acts can influence the character of a language; however, a language exists separately from any individual. In the same way, political actions (especially those that focus on symbols and ideologies) can influence established ideologies and the patterns of human interaction that those ideologies support.

This book argues that the success or failure of a minority political tactic needs to be evaluated not only for its success in achieving material or political gains for a minority group, but also from a larger societal perspective. The task of a minority political group is to rupture the ideological certainty of a society and an ideal that excludes the minority. For this reason, minorities in their political activities can function in certain circumstances as vanguards in generating ideological change.

Another reason for studying minority politics and minority political tactics is that in an age of growing interdependencies among nations, governments, economies, and other large bureaucratic entities, the psychological if not real position of more and more people becomes similar to that of a minority. Minority political tactics become relevant and possible as responses to encroaching and seemingly immutable economic, bureaucratic, and political forces.

While the political activities of minorities other than Blacks, Chicanos, and women also offer important insights into and challenges to traditional political ideologies in the United States, Blacks, Chicanos, and women all occupy particularly strategic political positions largely because of their histories and numbers. This does not mean that political activities of American Indians, American Asians, the handicapped, or other less populous minority groups are unimportant. They simply are strategically not as well situated to have impact.

Acknowledgments

The process of preparing this book began in the late 1960s when I was first hired to teach a course in minority politics. I am most grateful to the students I had in those years. We learned together. Colleagues who have been particularly influential and helpful in a variety of ways include Morton Auerbach, Sylvia Wynter, Ricardo Romo, Sondra Hale, Terry Winnant and Paul Goldstene. For help in preparing the manuscript, I want to thank Joyce Gerritson and Pamela Starr. W. L. Parker provided invaluable help as a perceptive copy editor. Finally, I am especially indebted to Howard Chandler for important editorial suggestions.

Minority Politics
and Ideologies
in the United States

Every established order tends to produce (to a very different degree and with very different means) the naturalization of its own arbitrariness. Of all the mechanisms tending to produce this effect, the most important and the best concealed is undoubtedly the dialectic of the objective chances and the agents' aspirations, out of which arises the *sense of limits,* commonly called the *sense of reality.* . . .

It is only when the dominated have the material and symbolic means of rejecting the definition of the real that is imposed on them through logical structures reproducing the social structures and [of lifting] the (institutionalized or internalized) censorships which it implies . . . that the arbitrary principles of the prevailing classification can appear as such . . . .

Pierre Bourdieu

Outline of a Theory of Practice (1972)

Introduction

The politics of minorities or the powerless have often been ignored in the study of interest-group politics in the United States. Minorities are generally those who do not have the resources, skills, knowledge, or organizational base to create the kinds of dependencies that characterize the politics of such powerful monied interests as oil, banking, or agriculture. Studies that do discuss the politics of the powerless tend to focus on tactics the powerless use to achieve material or legal gains and evaluate success in terms of whether these gains were reached. While this study will discuss and evaluate such tactics, the most significant aspect of minority politics lies in the ability of minorities to alter the psychological, conceptual, and ideological syndromes that legitimate and maintain the character of widely accepted superordinate-subordinate relationships within the society.

Basic to this thesis is the assumption that the legitimation of authority in a society occurs through mechanisms and interactions that do not lie exclusively in the realm of articulated ideology but also include established patterns of interaction and equally important established patterns of nondiscourse and noninteraction. Formal sets of articulated assumptions that fit together with some degree of internal logic to explain and justify political authority are, if widely held in the society, supported by largely unconscious, unarticulated patterns of interaction, customs, and manners. In other words, universes of meaning correspond to and are supported by universes of practice. Each influences the other in that a change in one will induce a change in the other. Whereas the dominant have no occasion to recognize this fact in their political activities, the interrelationship between institutionalized or habitual interactions and articulated ideologies that justify such practices defines the context within which minority political activity takes place.

Minorities operate on two levels in contributing to political change. Because of their subordinate position, minorities can see the dominant and the dominant ideologies in a way that the dominant do not. They have a different perspective. In their political activities, minorities seek to challenge the legitimacy of traditional ideological assumptions by identifying internal contradictions within these codes and by emphasizing the extent to which these ideologies fail to conform to observed and experienced reality. Minorities recognize and play on the stake the dominant have in the subordinate's acceptance of dominant ideological explanations and in the minorities' acceptance of their own inferiority. To challenge the dominant ideologies can be a bargaining chip for obtaining advantages for the minority. It can also serve to delegitimate the dominant ideology in the eyes of at least some of the dominant. The minorities' insights and their critiques of the dominant coding of the society can become a vital source of creativity and innovation in the development of new and perhaps better justifications of political authority.

In the area of practice, minorities are more likely to contribute to political change. Minorities struggle to say "no" to an "other." In this struggle for a new identity they seek to identify and disrupt everyday interactions, practices, customs, language, and habits that define them as inferior and subordinate. The refusal to accept subordination in a variety of what may seem to be insignificant ways can be an extremely important mechanism for instigating social, political, and ultimately ideological change. The very denial itself is a creative act. It is a quest.

Minority groups in American politics are closely bound to existing dominant ideologies. In their political actions, they do not break completely from the dominant's ideals but instead live with a multitude of conflicting identities. Because of their position, minorities are compelled to quest for a different ideal, a different truth, a different reality. Their politics are meaningful primarily in ideological terms. To participate in altering the ideals and attitudes of the society may be a more significant political achievement than becoming personally powerful in the traditional sense of "controlling" violence, goods, organization, and symbols. What makes minorities unique and creative is their very attempt to recognize and expose the existing ideologies as false ideals. They may do this on many different levels, beginning with personal everyday interactions and habits. Their search for human dignity attempts to peel away the obfuscating layers of a dominant's ideal. In so doing, their situation becomes a model and their quest becomes an ideal in itself.

Chapter 1

The Ideological Frameworks within Which Minorities Operate in the United States

To appreciate how minorities in United States politics challenge dominant ideological codings of the society, different systems of ideological assumptions must be delineated. The development of ideal types is the best way to cope with this problem, although any such categorization will necessarily obscure many differences and disagreements among those grouped within one category. Two ideological ideal types are most descriptive of the sets of assumptions that justify and explain the political world and political behavior in the United States today. These are the Lockean Liberal and the Pragmatic Utilitarian positions. The Marxist position is widely understood in the United States although it functions more as a critique of the other two dominant ideologies rather than as an ideology in and of itself.[1] (An ideology, as the term is used here, is a set of assumptions widely held in the society which fit together with some degree of internal logic to explain and justify political authority.)

The Liberal Tradition

The Lockean Liberal and the Pragmatic Utilitarian ideologies are liberal ideologies in that they both hold that government is legitimized not by tradition, or by God, or by God's spokesman on earth, but by the natural right of individuals to seek their own self-preservation.[2] (The term *liberal* here has a specific content and does not refer to the opposite of *conservative*, where "conservative" refers to the desire to maintain the current situation or return to that of a previous era.) The fundamental difference between the Lockean Liberal and the Pragmatic Utilitarian ideologies on this issue lies in the definition of self-preservation. The Lockean Liberal holds that self-preservation is equivalent to the individual's ability to acquire property. The Pragmatic Utilitarian, in contrast, believes that self-preservation must be defined by the individuals involved in a society as they interact among themselves according to democratically agreed-upon procedures. Other distinctions follow this basic difference.

The Lockean Liberal Framework

The writings of John Locke, a seventeenth-century English philosopher, explain many of the major assumptions of this ideological position, which is often referred to as "classical liberalism."[3] Locke believed firmly that the authority of government derives from the inalienable right of each individual to preserve himself by acquiring and accumulating property. Property, especially in the form of food, is essential to survival. Because Locke perceived the state of nature to be a hostile place where men are at war with one another, he reasoned that men joined together in a social contract to form a government in order to protect their right to acquire property. Government was and is, in this view, a basic instrument of individual self-preservation. The major function of government is to provide a political order in which the right to acquire property is protected. A critical concern of Locke's was that this government should not become tyrannical. Government should be limited in function and republican in structure, and it should include constitutional provisions for a separation of legislative and executive powers to help prevent tyrannical tendencies.

For Locke, the state of nature is one of unlimited resources. By using their labor, men can acquire property from the state of nature and make it their own. This acquisition is beneficial to the entire society. Government is necessary to protect this accumulated property as well as to secure the individual's right to acquire it. Since some men are more industrious than others, the acquisition of property will be uneven; some will have more than others. This difference is fine as long as there is no waste. Locke abhorred waste.

The use of money and the increased trade and commerce that a money economy allows become very important here. For Locke, money enables

1. The Ideological Framework

an individual with a surplus of nondurable goods to distribute those goods to consumers in exchange for a durable store of wealth, namely money. The industrious man who produces a great deal is thus an important resource for the society as a whole. In exchange for the accumulation of wealth, that individual enables many less productive individuals to enjoy the fruit of his labors. Everyone in the society is better off than before. (Modern commentators refer to this opinion as the "trickle-down" theory.) The Lockean Liberal position consequently privileges productivity, industry, efficiency, and ultimately wealth. The ownership of wealth or property indexes individual merit according to the Lockean ethic's assumptions and values. Those without wealth are obviously either lazy or inefficient. The Lockean Liberal position gives little status to the nonproductive, the poor, the lazy, the inefficient, and the helpless. The only political claim that minorities have in the Lockean framework is a right to equal treatment under the law as individuals and the right to acquire property. There is no provision for participation in the making of the law.

The Pragmatic Utilitarian Framework

The Pragmatic Utilitarian position draws on the ideas of a variety of political commentators, including John Stuart Mill and John Dewey.[4] The Pragmatic Utilitarian believes that self-preservation cannot always be equated with the acquisition of property. Instead, individuals in a society must decide what will lead to their own self-preservation in any particular circumstance. The role of government is to develop democratic procedures for assimilating all individual choices and acting to maximize the pleasure of all. The source of the government's authority lies not in a principle but rather in a procedure that allows all views to be expressed, debated, and evaluated. Minority expressions of self-preservation are vital for they may express a view that is essential to the well-being or even to the survival of the society as a whole. The Pragmatic Utilitarian assumes that men are by nature social and that they seek to communicate with one another to be mutually helpful. The role of government is to structure, facilitate, and regulate this process so as to insure that each individual in the society has an opportunity to participate.

Freedom of speech and freedom of association are especially important to the Pragmatic Utilitarian position, as are procedural mechanisms of voting and political participation. The role of government is a flexible one in which the distinction between the public and private depends upon how voters decide they want government to act. The idea is that the government should intervene in areas where its actions can eliminate pain or maximize pleasure for the greatest number. The private sphere, however, continues to exist for all activities that do not directly encroach on the consciously defined political rights of others. The Pragmatic Utilitarian is not willing to place production as the highest priority in privileging skills or individuals in the society. Depending on the circumstances, different skills and different people will be privileged at different times in history. In general, however, the individuals who can facilitate communication, who can broker interests, persuade, mediate conflict, and generate compromise will be highly valued.

Interest groups are extremely important for the Pragmatic Utilitarian as a means of articulating various interests in the society. Both powerful and minority interests are equally important to the governmental process and must be provided with an equitable voice. The Pragmatic Utilitarian position is the only major ideology in American politics that gives minority groups any claim to political legitimacy as participants in the political process. Minorities have used this ideological position extensively during the past century to push for more political voice and more political representation.

The Marxist Position

The Marxist ideological framework does not function as a major ideology in American politics but serves as an extremely influential critique of the liberal assumptions involved in both the Lockean Liberal and the Pragmatic Utilitarian positions. The Marxist position argues that the means of production determines the relations of production in society.[5] Capitalism continues to function as the dominant mode of production in the global economy as well as in many national economies, including that of the United States. Those who control capital constitute the ruling class. The governments of nation states are instruments of this ruling class, as are the liberal ideologies outlined above. While it is not clear whether the ruling class actually believes these liberal ideologies to be true or simply uses them to manipulate the masses, the Marxist position is that these ideologies function to oppress the proletariat and all others who do not control the dominant means of production. For example, the liberal distinction between public and private is to the Marxist nothing but a ruse which serves to obscure the close, self-serving connections between government agencies and powerful private interest groups. For many Marxists, the proletariat provides the only resource for overthrowing the ruling class and bringing about a more equitable political situation. Minorities are important only to the extent that they come to see themselves as a part of the proletariat and actively engage in a class struggle that will result in the overthrow of the bourgeoisie.

The Inadequacy of Traditional Ideologies

A major premise of this book is that the dominant ideologies in American politics are increasingly unable to explain or justify political reality. They are unable to cope with an interdependent world where domestic and foreign politics are closely intertwined. Neither are these ideologies able to explain and justify the blurring of the public and the private which characterizes the expanding realm of subgovernment politics. The demands of national defense and a global economy create a particularly intense dilemma for the Lockean Liberal position, which would keep government limited in function. For Pragmatic Utilitarians, the unchecked political power of special public and private interests (especially global corporations) is the central dilemma. Both Lockean Liberal and Pragmatic Utilitarian commentators are forced into ignoring aspects of these dilemmas when they make policy recommendations to achieve their respective political ideals.

In contrast, those with neo-Marxist assumptions have no difficulty explaining the international structure of major productive interests in the world. The need for new markets, the need for new and cheaper sources of labor and the organizational requirements for a more hierarchical division of labor are historical forces that neo-Marxists expect to materialize. Similarly, the established patterns of cooperation among private interest groups and governmental agencies are phenomena that neo-Marxists expect to be widespread. For them, the state is the instrument of the ruling class in a capitalist society and should be recognized as such. The problem with neo-Marxist analyses is not a lack of conformity with reality nor the lack of an ideal. The Marxist ideal of political equity in a society continues to be attractive and desirable. The problem is the lack of hope for realizing such an ideal within the neo-Marxist framework. Class has little meaning to American workers. Furthermore, the example of socialist countries where a "proletarian" (or peasant) revolution has occurred offers little inspiration. Old repressive patterns of superordination and subordination persist in spite of the revolution. The relative lack of individual freedoms and civil rights in most of these regimes is unattractive if not repugnant to most United States citizens. In general, the neo-Marxist framework functions primarily not as an ideology but as an intellectual critique in the United States.

Minorities and Ideological Change

The argument of this book is that old patterns of interaction have to change along with ideological and economic changes for political equity to be achieved. In bringing these changes about, minority politics has a central role to play in building and forming a new integration of ideal and reality, especially in a time when the old traditional ideologies are losing credibility. As Harold Lasswell noted, minority politics is heavily involved with symbols.[6] Murray Edelman argues that minorities can expect symbolic but not material gains from their political activities. Edelman tends to dismiss these symbolic or token gains as inconsequential.[7] This view, however, underrates the significance of ideals, symbols, and psychology in a society and assumes that such ideals or psychological patterns have no impact on the way rulers must rule. While Edelman is probably correct in arguing that any particular minority will not be successful in becoming an elite by virtue of its political actions, he fails to recognize that ideological and symbolic changes in a society are politically necessary for historical change to occur. The argument here is that ideals, values, symbols and psychological patterns have a dynamic of their own that interacts with (shapes and is shaped by) the economic and institutional forces of history. Whereas the politics of nonminorities focuses primarily on violence, goods, institutions, and old ideologies, minorities occupy a politically strategic position in being able to generate new symbols, new ideals, new psychological relationships, and a new political consciousness. Because minority politics is symbolic politics, the established Lockean Liberal and Pragmatic Utilitarian ideologies define the arena of political action and political possibility for minorities.

The ideals of the traditional ideologies—freedom from political tyranny, freedom to acquire property, individual procedural rights, and an equal opportunity to participate in governmental decision-making— continue to be extremely important ideals for United States citizens. These ideals form the tactical base for minorities in United States politics. Minority tactics derive their political strength from the contradictions that develop in trying to make the dominant live up to their own ideals. At the same time, minority groups working within ideological systems based on individual natural rights have to fight the psychological and

1. The Ideological Framework

cultural impact of these ideologies which work to convince the minority individual that his or her situation is an individual and not a social or political problem.

Notes on Chapter 1

1. For a more elaborate and detailed discussion of these ideological frameworks, see Jane H. Bayes, *Ideologies and Interest-Group Politics: The United States as a Special-Interest State in a Global Economy* (Novato, California: Chandler & Sharp Publishers, 1982). Chapter 3.

2. Louis Hartz, *The Liberal Tradition in America: An Interpretation of American Political Thought Since the Revolution* (New York: Harcourt Brace Jovanovich, 1955).

3. John Locke, "Of the Dissolution of Government," and "Of Property," *Second Treatise of Government*, in John Locke, *Two Treatises of Government*, ed. Peter Laslett (New York: Mentor, 1960), pp. 454–477, 327–344, and *passim*.

4. John Stuart Mill, "Utilitarianism," and "On Liberty" in John Stuart Mill, *Utilitarianism, On Liberty, Essay on Bentham*, ed. Mary Warnock (New York: Meridian, 1970), pp. 251–321, 126–250. John Dewey, *The Public and Its Problems* (Denver: Alan Swallow, 1927).

5. For an introductory survey of Marxist ideas, see C. Wright Mills, *The Marxists* (New York: Dell, 1962), pp. 41–96.

6. Harold Lasswell, *Politics: Who Gets What, When and How* (New York: World, 1972).

7. Murray Edelman, *The Symbolic Uses of Politics* (Chicago: University of Chicago Press, 1974).

Chapter 2

The Significance of Minority Politics

The Position of the Subordinate

The study of minority politics or the powerless demands an examination of the context within which minorities live and focuses attention on fundamental symbolic and ideological relationships that exist between subordinates and superordinates. The character of this relationship is integrally related to the self-definition or identity of the superordinate. To confirm his or her own existence and the legitimacy of his or her superior position, the superordinate creates an identity for the subordinate. This identity tends to exist in binary opposition to the proclaimed identity of the superior. The self projects an "other" that is its absence, that which it is not. If the ruler is holy and blessed by God, then the lowly are damned, possessed by evil and by other supernatural, awesome, and sometimes secret powers. If the superior is physically strong, the subordinate is portrayed as physically weak. If the superior organizes his own psyche in the name of rationality and legitimizes himself through reason, then the inferior are those who are irrational or perhaps mad. If the ruler perceives himself as producer, his projection of the other is as lazy, sensuous, nonproductive, sick, or handicapped. The "minority" of minority politics is a minority that is not necessarily a numerical minority but rather is of minor status and is psychologically embedded in that position. In this sense, minorities operate as stigmatized individuals in a "normal" society. The stigmatized and the normal are inextricably connected to one another. The very definition or identity of the stigmatized is with reference to the normal. If the stigmatized individual can challenge his or her social and psychological identity, then the normal individual becomes vulnerable as well.[1]

Michel Foucault, in his study *Madness and Civilization*, discusses the way in which the treatment by society of the mad as a minority has changed in different eras of history.[2] During medieval times, the insane were allowed to wander about as a part of society or were consigned to ships to remove them from the towns, or were put in chains and thrown into prison along with criminals, beggars, and others. Madness was outside of judgment. It was an unknown power, perhaps to be feared but not systematically subject to judgment. Not until the seventeenth century and the "great confinement," which involved placing thousands in houses of confinement, did the notion of insanity as irrationality become differentiated from other states of being. The development of the Age of Reason brought with it a gradual reflection of irrationality in the images used to explain and categorize the "other." Generally, the mad were separated from the poor, the criminal, and the sick. Foucault goes on to explain how "rational" treatment of the mad evolved. Whereas the eighteenth century attempted to treat the body, the nerves, and the fibers, and convince the madman of his madness, the nineteenth century sought to develop an internally conditioned mental control within the patient. The keepers removed the chains and instead applied the cold shower as punishment for every transgression. The patient became aware that he or she was being watched, judged, and condemned at all times. The effect was to induce, at least in some, an internalization of guilt, a self-alienation, a self-image of guilt and self-condemnation. Those who were not amenable to this form of socialization, those who continued to steal, to incite others to disobedience, or to refuse to work remained in chains.[3]

Foucault's insights concerning the mental and psychic shaping of a particular outcast and the relationship of the character of this shaping to the dominant mode of social discourse apply to minorities in modern society. Perhaps the most revolutionary aspect of minority politics in the twentieth century is the growing recognition by minorities of the extent to which they are imprisoned by their acceptance of a repressive self-identity that is reinforced by the symbols, practices, language, and personal habits of their everyday lives. In a society where production and the accumulation of property are honored, where the politics of the powerful revolves around strategies designed to obtain economic advantage in the control of goods and resources, minorities have found themselves politically impotent, not only because their strategic position gives them limited economic leverage but also because their psychic condition of alienation, self-hatred, and guilt constitutes an enormous barrier to effective political action. The minority leader must wage battle on two fronts. The tactics that are effective in dispelling psychic malaise often are not the ones that are most effective in achieving specific political or economic gains.

As with the politics of oil, agriculture, money, or any other set of interactions, the context within which various minorities attempt to establish and use dependencies is peculiar to the minority, its history, and its situation. The strategic positions and dispositions of the various minorities will vary accordingly and should be studied individually. In general, the tactics minorities pursue fall under three general categories. The first concerns tactics that emphasize the negative power of the minority; the second is a breaking-out tactic; the third focuses on creating dependencies. All three are concerned with ideologies, symbols, and values. Of the three, breaking-out tactics are the most ideologically innovative and even revolutionary. They must work hand in hand with dependency-creating tactics if minority politics is to make an ideological contribution to the society. Negative-power tactics are not revolutionary at all. Instead, they act to reinforce the existing ideological codes. Each of these tactics deserves some discussion.

Negative-Power Tactics

Tactics that involve negative power are those which do not publicly challenge the social identity or status of the minority in the society, but instead seek to play on the ruler's psychic need for confirmation and legitimation of his own superiority. The subordinate receives economic or status benefits in exchange for his or her submission to and voluntary recognition of the superior's authority. The use of negative power is more often an individual than a collective action, although its use may establish a widespread pattern in any society.

Perhaps because of their close integration at all levels of society, women have been prominent users of negative power. Instead of fighting for a change of status, many women have accepted their status and emphasized the advantages that such a confirmation of male dominance can bring.[4] The use of negative power involves understanding, accepting and manipulating the psychic needs of the dominant. Children, servants, prisoners, and the like are other categories that have traditionally employed tactics of negative power in an effort to survive.[5] By creating personal or psychic dependencies, the subordinate often can influence the decisions of the dominant, or in other instances, acquire a higher status simply by being closely associated with the dominant. The loyal and loving wife, the dedicated servant, the clever and adorable child, the unfailing secretary, the aging parent, the younger and weaker sibling, all develop ways of indirectly influencing the behavior of those who officially or psychologically dominate them by using their knowledge of the superior's own self-image and his or her own ideals and values. Goffman, for example, discusses strategies of information control which the stigmatized as individuals use in the exercise of negative power.[6]

In less intimate situations, the minority individual may acquire status in the eyes of his or her peers or may gain particular economic rewards in exchange for a nonhostile attitude and a ritual acceptance of inferior status. The prison trusty and the house slave as opposed to the field slave in American slavery are the most dramatic instances of this kind of negative power.[7] In each of these cases, it is fairly easy to see why the subordinate could accept the benefits of his or her position and yet maintain an inner attitude of rebellion and hostility. Such individuals might express attitudes of subservience toward prison guards or white masters while inwardly planning to escape. In such situations, the minorities play on the superior's need for a ritual acquiescence to obtain other benefits. Negative power, however, exists whether or not the minority is consciously seeking to break out of the identity imposed by the dominant.

The significance of those who use negative power is not the goods and resources they command; rather, their political importance derives from their patterns and habits of thinking that are alien to the dominant. The subordinate is of necessity forced to study and understand the weaknesses, inconsistencies, and motivations of the superior, who does not view himself in the same way. The dominant establishes a set of assumptions to explain and justify his own superiority and tends to believe those assumptions. Since he or she has physical force or other resources to maintain the asymmetric relationship, the tendency of the dominant is not to understand (or in many cases not to be able to understand) the thinking or the behavior of the minority. Black Americans have traditionally claimed to be able to understand whites better than the whites understand themselves. Women often make the same claims about men that servants make about their masters.

Breaking-Out Tactics

Breaking-out tactics are those that specifically challenge the image of the subordinate imposed by the dominant. Breaking-out politics recognize and address the content of the outward mask assumed by those exercising negative power. This kind of tactic proclaims the power of the

2. The Significance of Minority Politics 15

symbolic and the ideological and recognizes the extent to which *both* the dominant and the subordinate in any relationship are locked into a symbolic and ideological prison house. Breaking-out politics eschews the use of negative power. Instead, the strategy is to encourage the subordinate to recognize his or her own perspective, to articulate a new consciousness that will force the dominant to examine the contradictions in his or her own values, images and explanations. Grass-roots organizing, confrontation politics, and separatist movements are breaking-out tactics. Attacks on accepted symbols, images, concepts, ideologies, and explanations are important. History must be demystified, deconstructed, reresearched, and rewritten.

Breaking-out tactics involve articulating and communicating an experience of the world which is different from that of the dominant. The process is one of psychic self-confrontation for those who are minorities. The form of the process may vary. It may be organized, or may simply be spontaneous acts of rebellion such as absenteeism, rental defaults, voting, looting, the symbolic alteration of dress or behavior or speech. Frantz Fanon argued that acts of physical violence were necessary to break out of the subordinate mentality.[8] On the other hand, close group discipline, constant group reinforcement, a charismatic leader who in his words, deeds, and appearance constantly creates a symbolic ideal, are resources that have been used by both the Black and the women's movements in the United States. A systematic attack on various accepted uses of the language is a common breaking-out tactic. Terms of derision, such as "nigger," "bitch," "black," "chick," "chicano," may either be banned or else elevated as a source of group pride and group identity. The changing of names and/or titles, "Black" for Negro, "Chicano" for Mexican-American, is common. Religion has been extremely important in breaking-out tactics. Very often religion supplies a language, a set of rituals, institutions, and symbols which leaders can use to generate consciousness and identity. Feats of endurance and hardship by leaders, fasts, imprisonment, bravery in situations of extreme personal danger, all are tactics that help minorities to break out. If the leader is able to endure, to establish a new image and continue to survive, or if he has the conviction and confidence to be martyred, then followers are inspired to try.

Separatist movements tend to be the most explicit users of breaking-out tactics. A separatist movement declares itself completely incompatible with the existing regime. Emigration movements among Blacks in the United States are perhaps the foremost examples of separatist movements. Rapid changes in the economy, the population, or the social structure of the society due to war, famine, and disease usually set the conditions for breaking-out politics. It is in times of social disruption that traditional authorities tend to lose their legitimacy. Such conditions define the strategic situation for any minority just as other conditions establish the strategic situation for oil or agriculture or money politics. Social disruption often jars minorities out of a fatalistic attitude and into a general realization that social and political arrangements can change.

Dependency-Creating Tactics

A third kind of tactic employed by minorities involves organizing into a bargaining advantage for the minority the dependency of the dominant on the acquiescence or services of the subordinate. The use of the general strike by laborers is perhaps the most well-known and most often used example of how a minority can organize to bargain with the dominant. Other such bargaining tactics include the use of the economic boycott, the threat of violence and general disorder, the publicizing of gross contradictions between the reality of living conditions and the ideology of the existing regime. Civil disobedience, mass demonstrations, terrorist maneuvers, the mobilizing of voters, all are tactics aimed at creating a bargaining situation for the minority. In this kind of activity, the goals have specific and immediately definable objectives. The goals of the strategy and the possibilities for implementation are structured by the dominant ideals in the society as well as by the majority institutions and leaders. Dependency-creating tactics, although users may claim they are nonviolent, usually threaten disorder or disruption to the status quo by demonstrating to the dominant that the subordinates no longer accept established authority as legitimate. Minorities gamble on the structure of the ideology of the dominant.

In the United States the minorities operate within a context that is a combination of Lockean Liberal and Pragmatic Utilitarian ideas. Minorities engaging in protests, civil disobedience, and even violence base their activities on a faith that the dominant will give a greater value to the maintenance of production and to the rule of law than they will to repression; that the dominant will be tempered in their reactions by the arguments and reasons that they use to legitimize their own positions of authority in the society. In societies without a dominant set of ideologies based on the natural right of the individual to self-preservation, minority politics must take entirely different forms. The extent to which the dominant can use force and repression in the form of secret police, control of communications, control of education, confinement and/or execution of

2. The Significance of Minority Politics

dissidents in any modern technological society is largely a function of the ideologies and the institutions of the dominant. Because they have little access to economic or military resources, minorities must operate within the contradictions and interstices of dominant ideological structures.

The primary political resource of minorities in creating dependencies is based on a collective ideological determination to rebel by withholding services and/or purchases or by threatening disorder and violence. Many factors mitigate against the success of such political activity. Mancur Olson, for example, has described the very great difficulty which faces a group working for a collective public good that does not offer specific individual material benefits to those who are politically active.[9] Since the rewards of collective political action—such as consumer protection, civil rights, or women's rights accrue to all consumers, all Blacks, all Chicanos, all women, and all other minorities, the material incentive for the individual to be active does not exist. The minority simply has no material reward to distribute to individuals. The immediate individual rewards for political participation in a collective action must be primarily psychological, social, ideological, or perhaps even religious. Maintaining the unity of a group on the basis of ideological commitment is a very difficult task that is especially sensitive to the economic, psychological, social and historical circumstances of a given place and time. Very often the tactics required to maintain unity within the protesting group are precisely the opposite of tactics that would bring the most favorable immediate material or legal concessions. In some instances, minorities may aim to bargain with economic sanctions such as strikes, boycotts, and the threat of civic disorder, all of which reduce production and profit. In other instances, minority politics are primarily ideological in nature, aimed at playing on the contradictions within the dominant ideologies to attract third parties to the side of the minorities.

Because of these constraints, minority political leaders must be extremely creative. Michael Lipsky, in studying protest activities in urban areas during the 1960s, has argued that those minorities without economic resources must not only appeal to a variety of different constituencies but must also rely upon the communications media to attract third parties in the society to their cause.[10] Lipsky argues that any protest leader must appeal first to his or her own constituency, usually on the basis of some ideological position. Second, a protest leader must formulate arguments in such a way as to attract the coverage and attention of the media. The protest leader must pay attention to the kind of news, the kind of arguments that the media publish as they seek to maintain their viewing and reading audiences. A third constituency which a protest leader must attract consists of third parties. These third parties may be other political leaders or they may be the constituents of other political leaders. Finally, Lipsky argues, the protest leader must formulate goals and aim demands at authorities who can grant the demands or goals. For example, to demand amnesty from an individual with no authority to grant amnesty is to doom such a demand and perhaps the whole protest movement to defeat.

While Lipsky recognizes the ideological component of minority politics, his entire analysis suggests that minority politics is directed mainly at bargaining for material or legal resources and that "success" must be measured in terms of these material resources. While material gains are important in minority politics, such a definition of success does not do justice to the ideological component involved in such political activity. Politically active minorities must challenge a stigma that defines the minority not only in the minds of the dominant but also in the minds of many of the stigmatized minority members themselves. Rebelling against the stigma and against the code that defines the "normal" in terms of the stigma is perhaps more significant for social change than is the winning of particular material benefits. This does not mean that the minorities have an advantage in the use of symbols or ideological arguments in their political activities. The dominant who control material resources also control the media, the educational and socialization mechanisms of the society. Piven and Cloward, for example, argue that those who control the means of physical coercion and the means for producing wealth can and do channel protest for their own purposes; that the leaders and organizers of protest organizations unwittingly come to depend on dominant elites and that they allow the protest effort to be channeled by these elites into "normal politics."[11] They argue that the Kennedys channeled the civil-rights movement of the 1960s into electoral politics where Blacks were able to obtain the vote. However, even with the vote, Blacks can have only a marginal influence on improving the quality of their lives in terms of housing, income, and life chances. Both Lipsky and Piven and Cloward note that the dominant can and do respond to protest (1) by conceding token material satisfactions; (2) by appearing constrained in their ability to grant demands; (3) by using propaganda techniques to discredit the minority leaders; (4) by postponing action; and (5) by using superior symbolic material and coercive resources to redirect dissatisfaction into institutionalized controllable forms such as the electoral system.

In responding to challenges to the political status quo, politicians and other established leaders in the United States have used repression in

2. The Significance of Minority Politics

practically all of its forms. Terror tactics by police and vigilante groups, the censoring of communication, the use of public-relations techniques, the institutionalization of educational practices that deny information to certain groups, spying and eavesdropping, the harassment, the imprisonment, and/or the killing of protesters and dissidents, all are a large part of United States history. Yet the use of repression is mitigated somewhat in the United States by the ideological beliefs that even leaders and many of their staunch followers hold concerning the legitimacy of governmental authority in the use of repression.

The problem with this kind of assessment is that it deemphasizes the symbolic impact of minority politics. For Black Americans to obtain the right to vote, the right to sit in all sections of a bus, the right to go to an integrated school and to have the Justice Department engaged (if only sporadically) in securing such rights for Black Americans represents a significant change in the dominant ideology of the society. These may be symbolic concessions but they have important consequences that can influence the psyche not only of Blacks but also of whites. In this sense, the true significance of minority politics is not only the success or failure of any particular protest movement in achieving particular goals; it is rather the symbolic content of the protest as it is articulated by minority leaders in symbolic breaking-out activities as well as in actual bargaining or protest actions. This means that protest demonstrations, boycotts, and strikes are not the only forms that effective minority political activity takes. Separatist politics, propaganda, consciousness raising, and demystification activities are an essential aspect of minority politics. From this perspective, protest, strikes, violence and other overt activities aimed at obtaining material gains become "propaganda of the deed." The success of minority politics must be assessed according to the extent that these minority activities in fact deconstruct the dominant rituals and/or beliefs of the society as a whole.

The ideological significance of minority politics in the United States lies in the fact that minorities challenge Lockean Liberal and aspects of Pragmatic Utilitarian ethics in a variety of complex, subtle, and yet fundamental ways. Minorities in breaking out articulate a collective consciousness that undermines individual guilt and challenges social institutions and mechanisms that create that guilt. Minorities in the United States argue that individual identities are social creations, shaped more by the institutions and interactions of the society than by innate states of biological nature or supernatural forces. By articulating the parameters of their own alienation and "invisibility," minorities posit that not only they, but also their "superiors," are locked into a system that is not entirely of their own making. In this sense, minority politics is a form of doubting, a form of perpetual questioning. It is also a source of creative innovation. The significance of the political struggle of Blacks in the United States cannot be assessed only by examining changes in the distribution of wealth for Blacks, or by tallying changes in their legal status, although these gains are the most obvious. Its significance reaches beyond specific gains for a special interest group. It has illuminated and brought to consciousness aspects of the political system and the forces that structure it for the United States as a whole, not just for Blacks.

Ralph Ellison, in *Invisible Man,* writes of a Black man who in walking at night accidentally bumps into a white man. The white man insults the Black man, whereupon the Black man in a breaking-out state of fury assaults the tall blond man and demands that he apologize. The white man does not apologize. The Black man kicks, he hits, he butts, he prepares to slit the white man's throat, when suddenly he realizes that the white man has not *seen* him. He stops and lets the white man fall into the street. The realization is overwhelming. "Something within this [white] man's thick head had sprung out and beaten him within an inch of his life."[12] Ralph Ellison's *Invisible Man* is not just about the Black man in the United States. It is a novel about the society as a whole—Black and white, rulers and ruled. It is a scathing attack on Lockean ideals of individualism, hard work, the accumulation of wealth, and productivity. The irony is that the very calling of such ideals into question grows out of the Lockean and Pragmatic Utilitarian ideals themselves. The belief and expectation that the individual should exist as an individual and be recognized as such makes possible the frustration and outrage of an explicit recognition that this expectation is not met. The expectation is a myth that captures rich and poor, Black and white, superior and subordinate alike. By the same token, more explicit political activities of the Black movement have been important as a political education for both whites and Blacks.

The Strategic Situation of Minority Groups

The politics of various minority groups, like the politics of oil, agriculture, arms procurement, or health, exists within an historical context that shapes and structures the strategic situation for the minority. At any one time, certain minority groups have ideological leverage and are able to make more devastating critiques of dominant ideologies than can other minority groups. The strategic position of any minority group depends upon: (1) a degree of social disruption and displacement in the society, which creates disaffection and uprootedness; (2) the international political situation; (3) the content of the dominant political ideologies; (4) the ideological and political preparations that minority leaders have made in developing and articulating their own consciousness in light of the dominant ideologies; (5) the political skill of minority leaders in achieving symbolic as well as token material and legal concessions that can provide a stronger strategic base for raising consciousness in the future.

A degree of social disruption is essential to the success of minority-group tactics. In their thought-provoking study of protest movements, Piven and Cloward argue quite cogently that the strategic situation of minorities in politics is at best extremely weak in the United States. The possibilities for gain are circumscribed by the fact that disruptive protest is the most effective tactic for winning whatever can be won in a period of social disequilibrium. Disruptive protest as a tactic is further limited by the fact that once it begins to be successful, those who control the coercive and economic institutions in the society have a variety of resources available to dissipate and mitigate the protest: confrontation tactics such as physical repression, intimidation, and terror; diversion tactics such as opening up the electoral franchise, legalizing strikes, or appointing study committees; maneuvers such as the cooptation of unions and union leaders; deception through propaganda, especially through maneuvers to discredit leaders or to generate internal dissension within the minority organization. Yet even Piven and Cloward admit that within the boundaries of all these limitations, minority leaders and organizations make choices that are not completely structured by the situation and that have an impact on the effect of the protest movement.[13]

The international political situation is usually symbolically important for minority politics. It also may offer the possibility of generating third-party allies. The situation can be symbolically inspiring or discouraging. The experience is different for each minority. During the period from 1916 to 1940, Blacks in the Garvey movement made the liberation of Africa from European exploitation a central point of their ideology. The long-range strategy was to capitalize on European wars and on the discontent among colonized peoples around the world.[14] Similarly, Gandhi's successful nonviolent tactics, India's attainment of independence from Britain in 1947, and the achievement of independence by African nations in the 1960s all were important to the United States civil-rights movement as examples of people of color rising successfully against white oppressors. The Pan African conferences of the early twentieth century, the Garvey movement, the Black Muslim movement, the Black Panthers, and the Pan African movement of the 1970s and 1980s have all sought to build international linkages. Women in the United States have drawn inspiration more from the Black movement than they have from women's movements in other nations. Ideologically, however, many of the creative ideas that the women's movement embodies originated in England and France. The fact that over half the people in the entire world are women is a fact the women's movement cannot and does not ignore. The Chicano movement in the United States is clearly linked with economic and diplomatic relations between the United States and Mexico.

As has been stressed above, the content of the ideology of the dominant is particularly important to the strategic position of minorities. All three of the cases of minority political movements presented in this book have taken place in the United States since World War II, where the Pragmatic Utilitarian ideology is the only major ideology that justifies the representation of group interests as opposed to individual interests, although it also supports individual rights. Whereas the Lockean position holds that individual productivity, identified by the ownership of property, is what should sanction representation and participation in government, the Pragmatic position holds that all interests, regardless of productivity, must be represented for a good society to exist. Only through such comprehensive representation can the nation's public interest be defined adequately.

The latitude available to minority leaders is quite different from the latitude available to those with economic and coercive resources. The constraints are numerous. Timing is critical in choosing tactics. Dependency-creating tactics are governed by historical conditions for momentum and membership. Minority leaders must carefully weigh the legitimacy of their actions in light of the dominant ideology in a way that global corporations need not. A minority leader must balance breaking-out tactics (which maintain internal unity among his or her followers or which constitute creative new ways of thinking) against dependency-creating tactics that can secure more resources and negotiating leverage for the minority in coping with the dominant. Timing, judgment and creativity are essential. In spite of these disadvantages, the politics of minorities continues to be the locus of the quest for new dimensions of human freedom, a testament to the perpetually radical nature of the human spirit. This quality is the reason minority politics are significant, why they should be studied, practiced, and highly valued. Minorities are a major and critical link in a society's ability to transform and transcend itself.

Notes for Chapter 2

1. Erving Goffman, *Stigma: Notes on the Management of Spoiled Identity* (Englewood Cliffs, N.J.: Prentice-Hall, 1963), p. 135.

2. Michel Foucault, *Madness and Civilization: A History of Insanity in the Age of Reason* (New York: Vintage, 1973).

3. Foucault, pp. 259–270.

4. In her study *Purity and Danger*, Mary Douglas illustrates the way that various societies associate persons in a marginal state in the society with both danger and power. The very existence of these people challenges established perceptions of the social order and authority. She states: "So many ideas about power are based on an idea of society as a series of forms contrasted with surrounding non form. There is power in the forms and other power in the inarticulate area, margins, confused lines, and beyond the external boundaries." Mary Douglas, *Purity and Danger* (New York: Praeger, 1966), p. 98.

5. Stanley Elkins argues that the "yassuh, Massa" stereotype of the Black slave in the United States is not unlike the reported behavior of survivors in the Nazi prison camps of World War II. While Elkins has been attacked for considering the stereotype to be a reality, he does raise an important issue concerning the forces that impinge on the psyche of a dominated group. Stanley Elkins, *Slavery: A Problem in American Institutional and Intellectual Life* (New York: Grosset and Dunlap, 1963).

6. Goffman, pp. 41–125.

7. Another example in literature is Dr. Bledsoe in Ralph Ellison's novel *Invisible Man* (New York: Vintage, 1972), pp. 34–148.

8. Frantz Fanon, *The Wretched of the Earth* (New York: Grove Press, 1963), p. 94.

9. Mancur Olson, Jr., *The Logic of Collective Action* (New York: Schocken, 1965).

10. Michael Lipsky, "The Politics of Protest," *American Political Science Review* 62 (March 1968): 1144–1158.

11. Frances Fox Piven and Richard A. Cloward, *Poor People's Movements: Why They Succeed, How They Fail* (New York: Pantheon, 1977).

12. Ellison, p. 8 (note 7 above).

13. Piven and Cloward, p. 37 (note 11 above).

14. Emory J. Tolbert, *The Universal Negro Improvement Association of Los Angeles: A Study of Western Garveyism* (Ph.D. dissertation, University of California, Los Angeles, 1975. p. 47).

Chapter 3

The Minority Politics of Black America

The history and literature of Black Americans in the United States constitute the richest source of minority political thought and tactics that exists in the country. The historical strategic position of Blacks in the United States is unique. Unlike other ethnic groups that came to the United States more or less voluntarily, Blacks were initially brought to the United States as slaves and defined as property in the laws and basic institutions of the nation. The struggles against this initial status have constituted a major force in the political history of the United States, have been a major factor in a civil war, and in a multitude of ways continue to articulate the gross contradictions that persist in the Lockean Liberal ethic. Ideologically, because Blacks were defined as property, Black Americans occupy a unique strategic ideological position. The fact that Black Americans constitute around 12 percent of the population is another factor that gives Black protest more clout than the protest of other historically unique minorities, such as the American Indian. Black Americans have been an integral part of United States history. They have participated in the building of what is now the United States from the very beginning. Because they are such an integral part of the country, their protest as a minority is ideologically potent.

The forms Black protest has taken have included slave revolts, armed rebellion, individual escape to the North, emigration to Africa, Canada, the West Indies, South America, or elsewhere, martyrdom, and rioting, as well as protest and agitation in bargaining for particular gains such as enfranchisement, desegregation of public accommodations, equal schooling, equal treatment in the courts, and equal treatment in the marketplace. In evaluating the "success" of these various tactics, analysts look to the concrete material and legal gains which each protest effort produced to identify cause-and-effect relationships. Yet, the impact of Black protest has not been a linear one. A political strategist might assess separatist movements as politically ineffective, because even if a few thousand individuals do "escape" the conditions of the United States, no concrete material gains accrue to the majority of Black people who have not emigrated. Neither mass emigration nor territorial separation would ultimately materially benefit Black Americans. This kind of materialist assessment, however, misses the fundamental insights that Black minority politics offers. Minority politics *has* to be a psychological and symbolic struggle when all instruments of coercion and economic production are controlled by others. Engaging in armed rebellion can have a psychological impact on both whites and Blacks; however, unless the armed rebellion is carefully planned as a propaganda technique, or unless the legitimacy of the government is extremely fragile, armed rebellions by minorities tend to trigger repressive reactions against the rebels and everything they represent.

Repressive reactions cut off communication channels between and among minorities, instigate fear, and stunt any psychological or ideological development that might otherwise grow out of minority political activities. As alternative ways of pressing for political change in the United States, Blacks have developed and tested a variety of political strategies, each of which has been aimed in a multicentered way at deconstructing the dominant political ideology of the United States. No one strategy fulfills all the goals of the others, yet each builds on insights and perspectives that emerge from the Black experience in the United States. Other than armed or violent rebellion, three different kinds of political strategies characterize most of the Black movement in the United States. While considerable variation exists within these categories, Black politics can be understood as falling into (1) separatist movements and ideologies, (2) integration or bargaining ideologies, and (3) neo-Marxist strategies and ideologies. These movements and the ideologies that inspire them grow out of contradictions within Lockean Liberal ideals or else in opposition to those ideals. Only the integration ideology seeks legitimation in Pragmatic Utilitarian ideas.

Separatist Movements

Separatist movements have been an integral part of Black politics in the United States. Certainly the material and legal gains for Blacks that have been so painstakingly extracted from the dominant white society probably would not have been possible without the psychological and

3. The Minority Politics of Black America

symbolic impact on Afro-Americans that separatist movements have provided. Separatist movements have a psychological impact especially on the minorities themselves, while they do not incur the kind of repression that even the suggestion of armed rebellion elicits. As early as 1789, the Free African Society of Newport sent a proposal to the Free African Society of Philadelphia advocating a return to Africa as the way to escape the repression of the United States. An actual trip did not materialize until 1815, when Paul Cuffe, a wealthy Black ship owner, set sail for Sierra Leone taking thirty-eight other Blacks with him. This action was not threatening to whites; a group of white people in 1816 formed the American Colonization Society to help send Blacks back to Africa. The American Colonization Society made many free Blacks oppose the idea of emigration as they feared that the society's purpose was to make slaveholders more secure in the United States. James Forten, a friend of Cuffe's, wrote Cuffe in 1817 from Philadelphia telling him of the lack of support among Philadelphia Blacks for emigration but at the same time expressing his own private view that Blacks ". . . will never become a people until they come out from amongst the white people . . . ."[1] During the 1840s and 1850s, when the abolition movement was the commitment of many free Blacks such as Frederick Douglass, others like Martin R. Delany were calling for a return to Africa. In 1854, a convention of the best Black intellects met to lay plans for an emigration movement. Plans were made for exploring Central America, Africa, and Haiti as places to go.

The Civil War ended much of the separatist movement as the Emancipation Proclamation ended the legal institution of slavery and Blacks were elected to serve in Southern legislatures and in the Senate and the House of Representatives. An era of hope engulfed Black people in the South as federal troops enforced the Emancipation Proclamation and sought to repress the terror perpetrated by the Ku Klux Klan and other reactionaries. In 1877, however, this Reconstruction Era was ended by President Hayes withdrawing the federal troops, an action which gave white Southerners the upper hand once again. The Supreme Court in 1883 followed this action with a decision declaring the Civil Rights Act of 1875 unconstitutional. Segregation became the established policy, enforced by terror and lynchings in the South. Many Blacks moved from the South to Northern cities where they faced uprootedness, unemployment, continued racial discrimination, violence, and hatred.[2]

In the unrest of the late 1900s, Black leaders such as W. E. B. Dubois continued to articulate separatist notions even though their basic organizational strategies were designed to bargain with white society for material resources and equal rights. Booker T. Washington accepted the fundamental premise of the Lockean Liberal ethic that economics and politics can be separated. His famous Atlanta Exposition Address of 1895, which exhorted Blacks to develop basic manual vocational skills and maintained that "in all things social we can be as separate as the fingers on a hand" was segregationist more than separatist.[3] Dubois was more explicit in his articulation of the worth of Black people as distinctly dignified, strong, noble, human, and innately beautiful in spirit and soul. For Dubois, the Negro race possessed all the qualities that the Lockean Liberal's aggressive, productive, ruthless, materialistic ideal negated. To articulate the virtues of the negated "other," to develop pride in being black, to fight for the name of *Negro* rather than *negro*, and to launch a vigorous attack on the psyche of both whites and Blacks through this kind of consciousness raising certainly was in keeping with many of the emigrationist movements of the nineteenth century as well as with separatist movements that emerged later in the twentieth century. During his lifetime, Dubois engaged in a pragmatic, multicentered politics that explored and invented a variety of political strategies. In addition to participating in integration-oriented activities such as the Niagara Movement of 1905, which opposed the strategy of Booker T. Washington and called for equal rights and equal education for Blacks, and in the founding of the National Association for the Advancement of Colored People (NAACP) in 1910, Dubois also participated in Pan African conferences in 1900, 1911, 1918, 1923, and 1927 held in European cities. The Pan African movement urged American Blacks to unite with their African brothers to oppose white imperialist oppression. Later in his life, Dubois became committed to Marxism and to the Communist Party.[4]

The Garvey Movement

Between 1870 and 1900, dozens of small companies and organizations attempted to buy ships and in other ways promote a "back to Africa" movement. All were short-lived attempts. The organization of the separatist ideal into a full-fledged grass-roots movement did not occur until the time of World War I and the emigration of Marcus Garvey to the United States in 1916. During the war, over 350,000 Black men served in the army and many saw combat in France. The expectations of equality brought on by the war, combined with the economic dislocations of the wartime economy, encouraged thousands of Blacks to migrate out of the South to the Northern cities. Marcus Garvey was a Jamaican printer who, prior to coming to the United States, had participated in printers'-union strikes in Jamaica and had traveled and worked in numerous South American countries. In addition, he had been to London, where he

3. The Minority Politics of Black America

attended lectures and read more about Black African history. Of particular importance to Garvey was Booker T. Washington's *Up From Slavery* (1900). Garvey returned to Jamaica from London determined to unify the Negro race. In 1914, he founded the Universal Negro Improvement Association in Jamaica and embarked on a program of establishing industrial vocational colleges similar to Washington's Tuskegee Institute.

Garvey arrived in New York in 1916, with his message of Black pride, Black unity, and Black hegemony. By 1917, he had organized the Universal Negro Improvement Association in New York, and had traveled through a large portion of the United States, meeting with Black leaders and audiences where he found a welcome reception for his separatist ideas. Within two months of its organization, the UNIA had over 1500 members. By 1920, the organization claimed a membership of more than a million, had more than 30 branches in the United States and still more in the Caribbean, Latin America, and Africa. Garvey's strategy involved a symbolic consciousness-raising campaign along with an economic self-development program for the race. Garvey exhorted his audiences to seek racial unity, to organize Negroes of the world into a massive organization that would not only free the race but also free the continent of Africa for the Negro people.[5]

Unlike the previous emigrationist movements, which had been primarily responses to the hopelessness of life in the United States for Blacks, Garvey's message called in aggressive, colorful, and flamboyant terms for a positive international Pan African movement. Previous Black leaders had spoken to large groups but had been able to organize only a small number to carry out a program of action. In contrast, Garvey inspired and mobilized the first large-scale grass-roots political organization of Black people in the United States. He did not preach racial hatred, but rather the necessity for racial independence and racial pride. He emphasized the glory of Black history and Black pride as well as the view that "Black is beautiful." Instead of being ashamed, Garvey called for Blacks to be proud of their history, their hair, their features, and their skin color. That the Negro have a nation and a country of his own was imperative. Negro self-reliance, self-respect, and particularly Negro organization were essential. In a speech on November 6, 1921, Garvey called for Negroes to arm through organization. "I am saying to the Negro people of the world, get armed with organization; get armed by coming together 400,000,000 strong. This is your weapon."[6]

Garvey went on to argue that Negroes have an advantage in organizing because Negroes, unlike whites, have a common cause of oppression and suffering. Whites will be split according to capital and labor and since there is no common cause between capital and labor, whites will not be able to get together. Garvey argued that Negroes have no need to be socialists even though "all of us are laborers." That fight is not the Negro's fight. Instead, Negroes belong to the "Suffering Party" and consequently occupy a unique position when it comes to organization.[7]

Garvey's argument about the peculiar and unique position of the Negro race is brought out again in his discussion of the image of God. "If the white man has the idea of a white God, let him worship his God as he desires. . . . We as Negroes have found a new ideal. Whilst our God has no color, yet it is human to see everything through one's own spectacles, and since the white people have seen their God through white spectacles, we have only now started out (late though it be) to see our God through our own spectacles. . . . We Negroes believe in the God of Ethiopia, the everlasting God, —God the Father, God the Son and God the Holy Ghost, the One God of all ages. That is the God in whom we believe, but we shall worship Him through the spectacles of Ethiopia."[8]

In conjunction with the Reverend George McGuire, an Episcopal clergyman from Boston who founded the African Orthodox Church in 1920, Garvey propagated the idea that "God was made in our own image —black." At the UNIA convention in 1924, McGuire advocated removing all pictures of white Christs and Madonnas and other religious figures and replacing them with Black Christs and Madonnas. While this position was not well received by other Black clergy, the psychological and symbolic nature of the move exemplifies Garvey's perception of the kind of consciousness raising that was necessary.

A second important aspect of Garvey's Universal Negro Improvement Association was its ability to communicate. Not only was he an extremely colorful and effective orator but he also depended heavily on his journalistic skills. In 1918, Garvey founded *The Negro World*, a weekly newspaper printed in both English and Spanish, which helped propagate Garvey's message throughout the many branches of the UNIA. In addition, Garvey provided pomp and color wherever he went. He wore elaborately decorated military uniforms and headgear. He organized colorful, spectacular parades and other such events. Even the practical business aspects of his program were often more significant for their symbolic than for their economic impact.

In addition to the separatist ideological message, Garvey's program also included a strong economic component. Garvey's plan was to extend Booker T. Washington's idea of developing an economic base for Negro people; however, Garvey argued that while Washington's leadership had been important, the ideal which Washington advanced for Negro people was not sufficient. Not only did the Negro seek industrial opportunity, but he also *had* to have a political voice. The purpose of developing

Black businesses in the United States was only to provide an economic base for emigration to Africa. To this end, Garvey started the Black Star Line and the Negro Factories Corporation. The Negro Factories Corporation developed a number of businesses—grocery stores, a restaurant, a laundry, a publishing house, and other enterprises. The Black Star Line, however, became a symbol that epitomized Garvey's message. Thousands of people were willing to buy shares in the all-Black corporation to purchase ships that would eventually take some people "back to Africa" to establish a base in Liberia from which Africa could be freed of European imperialism. In the first year, Garvey raised over $600,000 for the steamship line by selling stock for $1 a share. The steamship line purchased three old steamers. Unfortunately, the individuals Garvey recruited to run the company were completely incompetent. By 1922, the ships were lost and the company dissolved; and in January of 1923, Garvey was charged by the United States government with using the mails to defraud. He was convicted of the charge and sentenced to five years in jail. After an unsuccessful appeal, Garvey went to jail in February of 1925. His sentence was commuted in 1927 and Garvey was deported to Jamaica, where he unsuccessfully attempted to reestablish his leadership over the UNIA. In 1935 he moved to London, where he died in 1940.[9]

The Nation of Islam: The Black Muslims

While Garvey's UNIA did not prosper without his leadership, separatist ideas in the Black community found expression in another movement that broke away from the Moorish Science Temple in the 1930s. Led first by W. D. Fard and in 1934 by Elijah Muhammad, the Nation of Islam propagated an ideology which held that the white race had been created by Yacub—a Black scientist who rebelled against Allah. The white devils were given 6000 years to rule, a period that ended in 1914. The chosen Allah had to be resurrected from the mental death imposed by the white man. Muhammad was this leader, "the Messenger of Allah and the Spiritual Leader of the Lost-Found Nation in the West." In the catastrophic Battle of Armageddon, the white slavemasters' children would be destroyed.[10] The Muslims not only rejected Christianity as the white man's religion, but they also declared Allah to be the "Supreme Black Man." To awaken from the death imposed by the white man, Black people had to throw off the white man's religion and the slave names that whites had imposed on Blacks. Elijah Muhammad emphasized the importance of self-identity to his followers. He exhorted them to discard the names of "Negro" and "colored." He spoke of how his followers had no knowledge of self, but rather had a limited and alien knowledge imposed by the slavemasters' children. He argued that the Black people had to learn that they were the first people on earth and that they had to rise up, throw off fear, and fight to be independent. Whereas the psychological imprisonment had been recognized and addressed as a problem by W. E. B. Dubois and more explicitly by Marcus Garvey, the Muslims identified the problem of psychic alienation and the lack of positive self-identity among Black people in the United States as a major political problem. To escape the hegemony of the white slavemasters' ideas and symbols, separation was essential.[11]

Prior to 1945, the Muslim organization comprised around 10,000 persons. After the war, and especially in the 1960s with the organizing skills of Malcolm X, the Muslims grew rapidly, establishing temples in most of the major cities of the nation. The program of the Muslims, like that of the UNIA, advocated a policy of racial separation and economic independence. However, the Muslims did not advocate emigration. The Muslim ideal called for Blacks to create a separate territorial nation which would split off and be separate from the rest of the United States. The southern states were most often identified for this separation and Muslim businesses moved to the South to begin to implement the process. The Muslim program of economic self-sufficiency spawned a variety of Muslim restaurants, cleaning establishments, bakeries, grocery stores, and other small businesses, all of which formed an integral part of the Muslim movement.

The internal discipline of the Nation of Islam was of particular importance to the political impact of the organization. To be a Muslim required a commitment to observe a variety of religious rules, such as not eating pork, not smoking, not drinking, observing washing rituals, and maintaining monogamous marriage relationships. The discipline was strict. Many admired the ideas and the program of the Muslims but did not join the organization because of the discipline. The discipline helped to create a cohesive organization. Selling the organization newspaper, *Muhammad Speaks*, was another task of the membership as well as a way of distributing the ideas of the organization.

From the 1930s until 1960, the Nation of Islam spoke to poor Blacks and to those who were in prison. It was primarily a religion rather than a political organization. Malcolm Little first came in contact with the organization while in prison. Upon release from prison in 1952 he became a principal organizer and theoretician for the group, as Malcolm X.[12] He continued the Muslims' traditional emphasis on Black psychic liberation and Black pride but was innovative in that he oriented the organization toward political action. Not only did he use his unusual oratorical skills to raise Black consciousness, he also critically analyzed the political institutions of the United States to make Black people aware of the tactics white leaders employ to manipulate Blacks and public opinion. In this sense, he deconstructed dominant ideologies and beliefs. For Black communities and Black organizations he demanded self-control and advocated physical self-defense.

Toward the last part of his life in 1964, just before his assassination in 1965, Malcolm X traveled to Mecca and to Africa. Upon his return, his ideas became much more international in orientation. He rejected many of the Black Muslim teachings to embrace the Islam of Mecca, which held that the Last Messenger of Allah was not W. D. Fard of the Nation of Islam but was Muhammad ibn-Abdullah, the Prophet and the founder of Islam. Furthermore, the One God was God of all, not God of just the Black race. Instead of identifying the white race as the cause of Black oppression, he began to identify structural and ideological phenomena that encourage a "racist psychology in the white man."[13] The Christian religion was a major culprit, as was the capitalist form of political and economic organization. Although Malcolm X did not engage in any extensive analysis of the myths or symbols of the church, he associated Christianity with the global conquest by Western Europe from the Crusades to the present time of imperialism and colonialism. Symbolically, Christianity was the religion of slavery and of a slave mentality for Black people. To be a Muslim as a Black in the United States was to break away from that imagery, to distance oneself in name, identity, and religion from the slave culture of United States history. Black separatism became not an end in itself but rather a means for Black people to break out of their psychic prisons and to assert their own independence. Whites had to be excluded from Black organizations, not because whites were inherently evil but because they prevented Blacks from becoming self-aware.[14] To implement these new ideas, Malcolm broke with the Nation of Islam to start a new organization called the Organization of Afro-American Unity, an act which he expected would bring a violent retaliation from the Muslim organization. On February 21, 1965, while giving a speech at the Audubon Ballroom in New York City, Malcolm X was assassinated.

As a political activist and as a theoretician, Malcolm X made an enormous contribution not only to the Black movement in the United States but also to the understanding of minority politics and political change. He understood and made others understand the need to break out of the psychic prison house that white cultural, economic, and political institutions imposed on both white and Black. Although he preached economic and religious separatism to his own constituency, Malcolm was looking for third-party allies in the emerging nations of the Third World, as well as among militant white groups within the United States. He admired the courage of Martin Luther King, but believed that any integrationist reform movement which did not challenge the fundamental structure and organization of the capitalist system in the United States could provide no real solutions. Nevertheless, Malcolm encouraged his followers to work for less than revolutionary changes by registering, voting, and developing a traditional political base for Afro-Americans in politics. At one point, Malcolm stated that the stance of militant self-defense which his organization advocated for Black people was what made the nonviolent philosophy and tactics of Martin Luther King and other integrationist movements successful. Basically, however, he believed that the whole society had to change if Afro-Americans were to be able to control their own lives, whether in separate Black communities or not.

Integrationist Movements

Black leaders who have advocated integration rather than separatism for Blacks in the society have tended to concentrate much more on the psychic, symbolic, and ideological state of white Americans than on the psychic liberation of their own followers. The strategy for integrationists has traditionally been to try to find and develop leverage for people in bargaining for a more equitable distribution of goods and services. To do this, Black leaders must locate and dramatize the dependencies that whites have on Blacks. Because Blacks do not control any aspect of the productive process and have no access to coercion as a group, integrationist strategies seek to exploit inconsistencies within the ideological principles of the white society, while brandishing the threat of unrest, disruption, and violence as the ultimate bargaining chip. Like separatist politics, integrationist movements are extremely dependent on a situation of social dislocation that disrupts both Blacks and whites from their feelings of complacency with ordinary routines. Around the turn of the century, Booker T. Washington was one of the first Black leaders to formulate a political tactic and philosophy for dealing with whites. Recognizing the fears which whites had of Blacks, especially in the South, Washington chose a strategy which conformed to the Lockean Liberal assumption that economics and politics are separate. Washington argued that Black Americans should not concern themselves with political rights and privileges but rather should attempt to build an economic base in developing manual skills that could enable Blacks to become self-sufficient economically. The Tuskegee Institute, founded by Washington, concentrated on teaching Blacks basic vocational skills. In his famous address at the Atlanta Exposition in 1895, Washington spoke not only to his Black followers but also to concerned whites when he advised Black people to consider themselves like the mariners who had become lost on a ship at sea and without water. At last, the lost ship saw another ship and signaled for help. The reply from the other ship was "Cast down your buckets where you are." Not understanding, the distressed ship signaled again: "Water, we need water." Again came the same answer, "Cast down your buckets where you are." Still incredulous, the ship's captain cast down the buckets and brought up fresh water, for the ship was in the mouth of the Amazon River. Washington urged his followers to cast down their buckets into the traditional skills and strengths of the Black people in the United States rather than immediately attempting to become professionals, senators, or congressmen and to enter other high-status occupations. As mechanics, gardeners, cooks, skilled laborers, Black people could establish an economic base for themselves.[15]

The National Association for the Advancement of Colored People

In opposition to Washington's philosophy, W. E. B. Dubois also preached an integrationist goal in the early 1900s; however, Dubois recognized and addressed the psychic problem of being Black in the United States. Dubois called for a policy that would encourage the most talented Black individuals to become educated leaders, doctors, lawyers, and politicians. Dubois called these individuals the "Talented Tenth" who would provide examples and role models for other Black people in their struggle to cope with white society. Led by Dubois, a group of Black intellectuals organized the Niagara Movement in 1905. Dubois argued that the state of the Black people in the United States was not the fault of the Black people themselves but rather was an oppression perpetrated upon Blacks. The Niagara Movement called for equal voting rights for males, equal economic opportunity, full civil rights, and the opportunity for Black youths to be educated according to their abilities. By 1910, the philosophy of the Niagara Movement was organized more formally into the National Association for the Advancement of Colored

People (NAACP), an integrated organization devoted to pressing for equal rights for Black Americans through the courts and as a lobbying group.[16]

Since 1910, the NAACP has achieved a number of remarkable successes through bringing cases to court.[17] In 1915, the Supreme Court declared "grandfather clauses" illegal.[18] These were legal devices that had kept Blacks from voting in the South. In 1917, the Supreme Court declared unconstitutional municipal ordinances that required Blacks to live in segregated parts of town.[19] Still another favorable decision came in 1923, when the Supreme Court overturned a murder conviction of a Black person because Blacks had been excluded from serving on the jury.[20] In the 1940s, the NAACP won important desegregation cases involving the equalization of teachers' salaries and school facilities for Black and white children in the South.[21] The Court ruled that dining facilities on interstate carriers had to be integrated[22] and that Blacks had a right to register and vote in Southern primaries.[23] The most famous and important case the NAACP supported was *Brown* v. *Board of Education* in 1954, where the Supreme Court overturned the "separate but equal" philosophy of the *Plessy* v. *Ferguson* decision of 1896 to declare that separate schools were not equal.

The NAACP has continued to press its campaign for the integration of schools throughout the nation. In 1939, the organization split into the NAACP Legal Defense and Education Fund, which engages in legal prosecution and defense, and the NAACP itself, which maintains a lobby in Washington, engages in research for documenting discrimination, lodges protests with those leaders in a position to do something about a problem, and in general comes to the aid of Black organizations and individuals that call for help.[24] The philosophy of the organization is one aimed at extolling accepted ideals of white American society—the sanctity of the rule of law, the right to equal treatment under the law, and the right to demand specific changes in the law and its administration. The strategy is to try to make the white government live up to the ideals it employs to justify its authority. It is a form of ideological politics. The relative success of such tactics depends heavily on the beliefs of those white leaders who make the major political and administrative decisions in the society. Violent and brutal repression of dissent is always available to those who control military and economic resources and is mitigated mainly by the beliefs and ideals of established leaders and the justifications they use to legitimize their own authority. A second important contributor to the self-defined success of such ideological tactics is the presence in the society of a much more militant group that makes more ambitious and more threatening demands. The threat of unrest, disruption, and violence and the subsequent erosion of political support for established leaders is the major bargaining chip of minorities in attempting to obtain specific goals.

The legal achievements of the NAACP did not occur in a vacuum. Large-scale economic changes in the nation, involving the mechanization of agriculture, helped to encourage many Southern Blacks to seek a better life as wage-earning workers in the Northern cities. In 1910, 80 percent of the Black population were engaged either in agriculture or in domestic service. By 1960, this figure had shrunk to 25 percent. Migration statistics also illustrate the changes that provided the background for Black minority politics during the twentieth century. In 1900, over 90 percent of the Blacks in the United States lived in the South. By 1960, only about half of the nation's Black population remained there. The rest had moved north or west to form large concentrations in urban areas. This kind of uprootedness and disruption of rural agricultural life was occurring also among white farmers, as growing industries employed more and more workers.[25]

The Union Movement and Black Workers

Another integrationist organization formed at about the same time as the NAACP was the National Urban League. Founded in 1912, the Urban League focused its attention on finding jobs for the migrant Black worker and attempted to facilitate the adjustment of Blacks to urban life. Like the NAACP, the bulk of the support for this organization came from white donors. While advocating integrated trade unionism, the Urban League did little else to fight the racial discrimination that pervaded the American Federation of Labor and the trade union movement as a whole. By 1920, Black workers had begun to organize their own locals. In 1925, A. Philip Randolph finally organized the first Black union, the Brotherhood of Sleeping Car Porters, and was able to get the support of both the NAACP and the Urban League in his drive to integrate the trade-union movement.[26] From this position, Randolph launched a number of attacks against the racial discrimination of the American Federation of Labor. In its earliest days, this organization had genuinely been committed to racial equality; however, in the 1890s under Samuel Gompers, it had switched to a policy of advocating equality while sanctioning inequality and discrimination. The Communist Party was also fairly active during the 1920s and early 1930s in attempting to organize Black workers, especially in the South. The Communists were able to organize a number of groups such as the American Negro Labor

Congress, the Sharecropper Union, and the integrated Trade Union Unity League. For awhile, Langston Hughes was the president of the League of Struggle for Negro Rights. In 1933, the League organized a march on Washington of about 3500 people to give President Roosevelt a Bill of Civil Rights for the Negro People.[27]

Some definite material advances resulted from these activities. Randolph was able to get full bargaining power for his union in 1937 and obtained about $1.5 million in salary increases for his 8000 members.[28] The Congress of Industrial Organizations, founded in 1935 to organize unskilled industrial workers, was much more militant in advocating equality for Black workers than the American Federation of Labor, although this militancy was short-lived. The Communist Party, in spite of its attempts to project an ideology of worker solidarity, did not capture the imagination of either Black or white workers in the way that its leaders had hoped. After growing to a membership of over 70,000 during the 1930s, the Party began to decline in membership and appeal with the entry of the United States into World War II.[29]

Direct Nonviolent Mass Action: CORE, SCLC, and SNCC

The idea that direct nonviolent mass action could be used successfully to desegregate eating establishments, transportation, and housing was the belief and purpose of the Congress of Racial Equality (CORE), founded in 1942 by a group of Blacks and whites. James Farmer, a former Methodist minister, was among the founders and was the first national chairman of the CORE.[30] Although it was in existence in the 1940s, and had some local success desegregating housing projects in New York and Chicago, CORE had little visibility until the 1960s.[31] The first major event which represents the beginning of the Black nonviolent direct action campaign of the 1950s and 1960s came on December 1, 1955, in Montgomery, Alabama. On that day, Mrs. Rosa Parks refused to obey the bus driver when he demanded that she give her bus seat to a white man. Mrs. Parks was arrested and the entire Black community was spurred to action by the outrageousness of the event. Meeting on the night of December 2, a large group of Black leaders decided to call for a bus boycott—75 percent of the bus riders in the town were Black. The group became the Montgomery Improvement Association with Martin Luther King, Jr., a young Baptist minister, as its leader.[32] The Montgomery Improvement Association, with the help of the NAACP, brought the case to court amid considerable local violence and terrorism committed against Blacks by enraged white citizens of Montgomery. The Federal District Court ruled on June 4, 1956, that segregated seating on municipal buses was illegal, a decision the Supreme Court upheld four months later. Out of the Montgomery experience, Dr. King mobilized another organization of clergymen from Southern cities, called the Southern Christian Leadership Conference (SCLC). The assumption of this organization was that clergymen were ready to lead the civil-rights movement with nonviolent direct protests. By 1960, the SCLC had about 65 affiliated organizations in various southern cities and was engaged in voter-registration drives, nonviolent-protest training, and even citizenship training.[33]

The next outbreak of protest came from students in Greensboro, North Carolina, who on February 1, 1960, walked into a Woolworth's store and sat down at the all-white segregated lunch counter. This sparked the second of the major nonviolent campaigns of the civil-rights movement and, with the help of CORE and SCLC, brought into existence the Student Nonviolent Coordinating Committee (SNCC), headed initially by James Forman. The Student Nonviolent Coordinating Committee drew support from both Black and northern white students to wage a series of sit-ins combined with economic boycotts and voter-registration drives in various southern cities such as McComb, Mississippi, Albany, Georgia, and Nashville, Tennessee. The success and daring of this new organization led the Congress of Racial Equality to become more active. In 1961 James Farmer, as head of CORE, launched the Freedom Rides to integrate bus-terminal facilities. The first Freedom Ride involved five whites and six Blacks who took a bus trip from Washington, D.C., through Atlanta and the Deep South to New Orleans. This began the Freedom Ride movement, which included about a dozen rides and involved hundreds of people. In spite of state police protection, the rides met bitter opposition from whites, including fire bombs, bus tires being slit, physical attack, and shootings. Many of the riders were jailed in Mississippi. By November 1961, the Interstate Commerce Commission had banned segregation in terminal facilities.[34]

The Theory of Nonviolence

The major theoretical exposition of the nonviolent direct-action protest movement embodied in the actions of SNCC, CORE, and SCLC were the most clearly articulated by Martin Luther King, Jr., during his campaign in April and May of 1963 to integrate the city of Birmingham. King had come to Birmingham at the invitation of the local affiliate of the Southern Christian Leadership Conference because, as he put it, "Birmingham is probably the most thoroughly segregated city in the United States."[35] After attempting to negotiate with the white leaders of the town, King applied for a parade permit to march in the city and was denied the permit. On Good Friday, King marched anyway and was arrested along with about 55 others. While in jail, and in response to public statement by a group of eight white Alabama clergymen deploring the demonstrations and calling for "working peacefully for a better Birmingham," King wrote the must lucid defense of his strategy and philosophy. This "Letter from Birmingham Jail" clearly demonstrates the delicate and complicated strategy that characterized all of the nonviolent direct-action protests of the period. King insisted that every nonviolent campaign has four basic steps: (1) the gathering of information to determine that injustices exist; (2) negotiation; (3) self-purification, and finally (4) direct action.[36] In following these four steps, nonviolent tactics are designed to play on the ideology of the oppressors.

It should be no surprise that nonviolence as a tactic has had any large-scale success only against leaders who believe in an Anglo-American legal tradition (British-ruled India and the United States). As with any protest action, the effectiveness of nonviolent action depends primarily on the use of ideologies and symbols. Through skillful political maneuvering, a nonviolent protest leader must appeal to at least four different constituencies. First, the leader must inspire his or her immediate followers. Second, he or she must be able to attract the media to communicate a message to still a third constituency, third parties—minorities, by definition lacking the goods or violence to obtain what they want, must attract allies by appeal to ideals, arguments, and symbols. Finally, if the aim of the nonviolent protest is a specific concession, then the leader's demands must be directed and constructed in such a way that the officials involved have the authority to grant the demands.[37]

Dr. King in his "Letter from Birmingham Jail" explicitly appealed to at least one third party—the white clergy of Alabama. He also appealed to third parties throughout the nation who believed in democracy and the rule of law. The most powerful of third parties, of course, was the federal government. In his letter, King stressed and conformed to the ideals of the dominant ideology in the United States while emphasizing the disparity between these ideals and the reality of Birmingham. King did not call for revolution; he did not call for a new form of government. Instead, he wrote of "just" and "unjust" laws. He argued that segregation laws are unjust laws, unjust morally, economically, and socially. Legally, they were unjust because Blacks did not participate in the making of those laws and the laws imposed upon Black people a legal code that did not apply to white people. King went on to argue that it is also unjust for perfectly just laws, such as the requirement for a parade permit, to be administered to preserve segregation and thereby deny to individuals their right to protest and assemble peacefully. In upholding the ideal of the rule of law, King maintained that any individual who breaks an unjust law must do it with a willingness to accept the penalty. King never asked for amnesty but rather attempted to use his jail sentences as a means of arousing the conscience of the community concerning the injustice of the laws that put him and his followers in jail. To be willing to accept the punishment for breaking the parade-permit law was to support a more important principle that the law should be obeyed.

Significant also in King's appeal to third parties is his insistence on negotiation and compromise. The whole purpose of direct action is to develop "creative tension" for the purpose of bargaining. The weapons Martin Luther King had in bargaining with Birmingham city officials were the unified organization and purpose of his own immediate followers, the purchasing power of 300,000 Black citizens of Birmingham, and the moral argument combined with media-conveyed evidence that Birmingham's laws promoted and enforced segregation and were consequently unjust in accordance with traditional American political thought. Only when negotiation without the "creative tension" of direct action has failed does King argue that nonviolent direct action is justified. Nonviolent direct action is a way of making it clear to the leaders of Birmingham that their own position of leadership is at least in part dependent upon the acquiescence and cooperation of the Black population of Birmingham. King's third step, self-purification, is important here. For a minority, to threaten violence or economic boycott as a means of bargaining can be effective in some situations.[38] However, in a situation like that in the South, where the exercise of violence and terror by whites had been culturally institutionalized by slavery and its aftermath, and where whites clearly still monopolized the sources of physical and economic power, the strategy of violence could easily lead to more racial repression wherein the dominant whites would be fully self-justified in their own repressive reactions. The nonviolent strategy appeals to the dominant's own ideals of law and order, of equal protection of the laws. For nonviolent protests to be effective ideologically, the leadership must communicate both to the officials who are the object of the protest and to potential third parties the message that the protesters are unswervingly committed to the ideals of the dominant—more committed than the rulers themselves.

For King, self-purification was the strategy he used to inspire his own followers. In the most concrete sense, this meant developing the self-discipline not to react violently when provoked by taunts, jeers, and insults, by physical beatings, by having hot coffee poured down one's back, by having burning cigarettes placed on one's skin, or by being tortured with electric jolts from a cattle prod. Self-purification for King meant developing the inward physical and political strength to withstand such pain to achieve a higher moral purpose. Self purification also meant being willing to go to jail for breaking the law. Only by willingly accepting the lawful punishment for violating the law could nonviolent protesters convey to third parties that they were not opposing the rule of law as such, but rather were concerned about changing unjust laws. The tactics King used to unify and inspire his own immediate followers were historically conditioned. King was a Southern Baptist preacher. His followers had in common the Christian religion as Black people had experienced it both during slavery and afterwards. The Old Testament provided a great deal of the theoretical background for these immediate followers. The idea of a promised land, combined with songs of slavery, spirituals, prayer meetings, Bible study, and King's own preaching skills constituted much of the inspiration that motivated King's followers.

The impact of the civil-rights nonviolent protest action mobilized by SNCC, SCLC, and CORE during the 1960s was considerable, both politically and psychologically. The movement grew from a concern with integrating eating and transportation facilities by using the sit-ins and Freedom Rides in 1960–1961 to a full-scale attack on the system of desegregation in particular cities (such as Albany, Georgia, in December 1962, and Birmingham, Alabama, in April and May of 1963). The Birmingham protest ended with an agreement on May 10 that recognized the Black community by creating a biracial committee and a plan for the integration of public facilities and the hiring and promotion of Black workers in local businesses.

The bombing of SCLC headquarters in Birmingham a day later and the resulting riots by the Black community marked the beginning of a further escalation of the movement. The President finally ordered federal troops to Birmingham and threatened to nationalize the Alabama National Guard. In response, a new echelon of Black leaders in other parts of the country (among them Gloria Richardson of Cambridge, Maryland, and Cecil Moore of Philadelphia) began organizing their own followers using their own local resources to lead protest demonstrations.[39] These individuals developed new tactics that involved large numbers of people, stressed economic issues, and threatened large-scale civil disobedience.

In many instances, their demonstrations were more militant in tone than King's, as were the means used to repress the protests. Angry voices, including those of Malcolm X and James Baldwin, attracted the sympathies of many Blacks—especially the youth. Local chapters of CORE began taking the initiative to stage such acts of civil disobedience as holding a sit-in to block traffic on the Triborough Bridge in New York. During the summer of 1963, scores of demonstrations erupted throughout the nation.

What was becoming increasingly clear to both Black and white leaders was that the situation was well beyond the control of any one Black leader or group. Many of the youth looked on Martin Luther King, Jr., the NAACP leadership, and other bourgeois Black leaders as being not radical enough. The threat of an uncontrollable uprising of open civil disobedience across the country was very real. Presidential politics, Congressional elections, and the smooth running of the national economy, all were at stake. Confrontation politics on a massive scale was raising the hopes and aspirations of many Blacks as well as the deep-seated fears of many whites.

The policy of the Kennedy Administration was to encourage voter registration drives rather than desegregation confrontation politics. Kennedy had experienced the electoral advantage of appealing to Black voters in his 1960 Presidential campaign. In October 1960, just before the election, Martin Luther King, Jr., had been arrested for violating the terms of a 12-month parole sentence which he was serving for a previous minor traffic violation. In violating the parole, King had participated in a sit-in. The judge sentenced King to four months of hard labor in Reidsville State Prison in Georgia. King's supporters immediately appealed to the White House for help. Neither Eisenhower nor Nixon chose to intervene; however, Candidate Kennedy did. John Kennedy called Mrs. King while Robert Kennedy called the judge who had sentenced King. Martin Luther King was promptly released. The news made a tremendous impact in the Black community.[40] In analyzing the extremely close 1960 election, many commentators identified the Black bloc vote as crucial in winning the electoral votes of states such as Illinois and Texas, where the margin of victory for Kennedy was extremely small (around 5000 votes).

The Kennedy strategy, once in office, was to build support for the Democratic Party in the South by registering Black voters.[41] However, as Piven and Cloward have argued, the voter-registration drive sponsored by the Justice Department's prosecution of cases was countered by Kennedy's continued appointment of racist federal judges in the South.[42]

The crisis generated by the protest demonstrations in Birmingham encouraged the Administration to devote renewed attention to a civil-rights bill. Meanwhile, Black leaders joined with white labor leaders and other liberals to organize a March on Washington that took place on August 23, 1963, to demand federal legislation for civil rights and for social-services programs to benefit Black people). Spurred on by the September bombing of a Black church in Birmingham in which four young Black girls were killed and by the assassination of President Kennedy in November 1963, Lyndon Johnson committed his Administration to the passage of a civil-rights bill. This he finally signed into law on July 2, 1964. While this law provided some symbolic help, it had no provisions for enforcement. Obtaining such provisions became the next item for civil-rights protesters.

During the summer of 1964, SNCC, CORE, and the Mississippi branch of the NAACP conducted a voter-registration drive in Mississippi which involved sending hundreds of college-age civil-rights workers—both Black and white—into Mississippi to help register voters.[43] This drive was greeted with killings and bombings. At least five of these students were murdered. In the North, rioting occurred in Cambridge, Maryland, New York, Jersey City, Paterson, Philadelphia, and a suburb of Chicago. Determined to keep the pressure on the administration, King in January 1965 began a mass protest movement in Selma, Alabama, where voting-registration violations had been occurring. Thousands of demonstrators were arrested, most of whom were children. When a young boy, Jimmie Lee Jackson, was shot and killed, King called for a march from Selma to Montgomery. Governor Wallace prohibited the march and Alabama troopers confronted the marchers with tear gas, cattle prods, and clubs. President Johnson responded by federalizing the Alabama National Guard and ordering another 1862 guardsmen to protect the marchers along their route from Selma to Montgomery. The march began on March 21 with about 8000 people. Five days later, the group arrived in Montgomery and were joined by about 30,000 sympathizers. That night a white marcher from Detroit, Viola Liuzzo, was shot and killed. The national publicity that accompanied this march and the killing, combined with the violence that accompanied voting-registration drives in other parts of the South, made it clear to Congress that further legislation was necessary. By August 6, 1965, President Johnson was able to sign the Civil Rights Act of 1965, which authorized the Attorney General to appoint a federal voting registrar in counties that had maintained a test or other prerequisite for voting as of November 1, 1964, and that had a total voting age population wherein less than 50 percent had registered or voted in the 1964 presidential election.[44]

3. The Minority Politics of Black America

The Birth of the Black Power Movement

In 1966, dissension was beginning to grow within the ranks of SNCC, SCLC, and CORE. The 1965 Civil Rights Act, which was to have sent federal registrars to hundreds of Southern counties along with federal marshals to enforce the law and protect Black citizens, had not been implemented. Fewer than 60 registrars had been appointed and no federal law-enforcement officers had been sent to the South. Many who had previously had faith that the new laws would make a difference were bitterly disappointed. When James Meredith was shot and wounded while attempting to hold a March for Freedom in Mississippi, Martin Luther King, Jr., along with Stokely Carmichael of SNCC and Floyd McKissick of CORE, all flew to Memphis to visit Meredith and to continue the march that he began. It was at this time that both Carmichael and McKissick discarded King's nonviolent philosophy to promote the slogan of "Black Power." This turn of events deeply distressed King, who understood the frustration and the need for identity and self-pride which the slogan evoked. In his book *Where Do We Go From Here? Chaos or Community*, King writes at length of the positive aspects of Black Power in uniting, encouraging, and inspiring Black people to develop economic and political strength within the Black community and to keep themselves from being absorbed either culturally or politically into conditions of continued degradation and impotence.[45] At the same time, King argued that as a symbol, Black Power would have a very negative political impact. He believed that the Black Power movement, "like the Garvey 'Back to Africa' movement of the 1920s, represents a dashing of hope."[46] Black Power was born from disappointment and despair, disappointment that was very real and understandable in the face of the many setbacks and the continued intransigence of white America in the face of years of Black struggle and suffering. King went on to argue that revolution cannot be sustained by despair.[47]

Furthermore, King pointed to what he considered to be the impossibility of a "separate Black road to power and fulfillment." Alone, without allies, Blacks could not gain significant electoral power. Blacks alone could not exercise their economic power as consumers as significantly as if they allied themselves with all poor people or with all workers. Finally, King wrote that the call for self-defense by Black Power advocates implied a call for retaliatory violence that could easily be interpreted by whites as an invitation to aggression. For King, a violent rebellion by Black people in the United States meant a holocaust for them. Violence as a strategy for a minority in opposing a well-financed, well-organized government supported by loyal armed forces and the allegiance of the majority of its people could not possibly be successful in King's eyes. The riots had brought tremendous misery to Black people and only a few concessions. To hope that the two-thirds of the world that is "colored" will violently rise to overthrow white oppression was "beyond the realm of serious discussion."[48] Black countries were much too busy with their own internal affairs to be of any aid to American Blacks. In fact, ". . . the hope of the people of color in the world may well rest on the American Negro and his ability to reform the structure of racist imperialism from within and thereby turn the technology and wealth of the West to the task of liberating the world from want."[49]

In spite of King's opposition, the Black Power movement continued to grow in a variety of ways in 1966. Malcolm X had been assassinated in February 1965. Before his death, he had broken with the Black Muslims and was developing his own philosophy which emphasized self-defense and pointed to an international coalition with the African Freedom Movements. Malcolm's new organization was called the Organization for Afro-American Unity, patterned after the Organization of African Unity. In Louisiana, the Deacons for Defense and Justice organized to engage in self-defense against terrorism that still prevailed against Black people. Stokely Carmichael and SNCC organized the Lowndes County Freedom Organization in 1966, using the slogan of Black Power.[50] At the same time on the West Coast, Huey Newton and Bobby Seale were organizing the Black Panthers.

While all of these organizations were considerably different from one another in their constituents and in their specific programs, all borrowed heavily from ideas developed and articulated by Malcolm X. Robert Allen put it quite well when he called Malcolm the ideological father of the Black Power movement.[51] Malcolm had argued for self-defense and for Black control of Black communities and organizations. He had spent much of his career speaking to Black people to demystify some of the symbols and language used by whites in their writing of the nation's history. He had illustrated the extent to which the language and culture of whites in the United States continued to imprison both whites and Blacks. After breaking with the Black Muslim organization in 1963, he had agonized over the problem of whether separatism was still a necessary and viable policy for the freedom of Black people. He concluded that it was not racism as such but the structure of the society that generated both white and Black racism. Blacks were victims of domestic colonialism. For racism to dissipate, the economic system, the political system, and the social system had to change.[52] Finally, Malcolm brought to the struggle in the United States an awareness of and a concern for oppressed people in the rest of the world. He argued that Blacks should internationalize their struggle. The questions Malcolm raised helped to guide most of the organizations that participated in the Black Power movement, in the Afro-American Movement, and in the neo-Marxist liberation movements of the 1960s and the 1970s.

The Lowndes County Freedom Organization

The summer of 1966 was one of considerable political and social turmoil in the United States. In 1965, President Johnson had decided on open intervention in Vietnam. The escalation of the war brought a wave of protest demonstrations across the country, including a march of 25,000 antiwar demonstrators in Washington during the spring of 1965. Early in 1965, SNCC voted to join the antiwar forces and in January 1966 issued a statement opposing the war and supporting draft resisters. CORE also endorsed Black Power as a policy in 1966. In the context of these events and James Meredith's Freedom March, Stokely Carmichael and SNCC organized the Lowndes County Freedom Organization in Alabama, using the slogan of Black Power. While the major program of the Lowndes County Freedom Organization was one of building Black community solidarity and registering Black voters, the rhetoric and symbolism of the organization borrowed heavily from ideas developed and articulated by Malcolm X. Carmichael, in the book *Black Power*, which he wrote with Charles Hamilton, spoke only briefly about the colonialization of Black Americans and the need for revolution. He made it clear that Black people were no longer going to "turn the other cheek" in nonviolent protest but that they were going to fight back.[53] Carmichael also addressed the problem of the psychological condition of the Black people that the tradition of slavery still affected—the need for self-respect, self-worth, and self-dignity.

On the question of building political coalitions with white liberals, with labor unions, with the Democratic Party, with churches, or even with poor white people, Carmichael argued that the experience of the Mississippi Freedom Democratic Party (which had unsuccessfully attempted to seat a Black delegation from Mississippi at the Democratic National Convention in 1964) illustrated the futility of such coalitions at the time. The Mississippi Freedom Democratic Party had aimed at attracting political support from northern delegations to displace the all-white delegation. In his book, Carmichael noted that the Black community would always be dominated in any coalition with whites until Blacks were able to develop psychological equality and a power base of their own. For this reason, whites could not help in Black liberation activities. While not opposed to coalitions in the future, Carmichael argued that whites needed to contribute by educating other whites concerning the need for Black Power.

Clearly, the rhetoric of the Black Power movement as articulated by Carmichael was not revolutionary. It was militant only in comparison with Martin Luther King's nonviolent philosophy. Carmichael concentrated on the problems of organizing political voting power for Blacks within the existing system and tended to rely on help from the federal government as an ally whenever necessary. Because of race riots during the summers of 1964 and 1965 in the major cities of the nation, Carmichael's statements took on an added tone of reality when he predicted guerrilla warfare in the United States should the Black Power political tactics fail. Many moderates, both white and Black, were very much aware of the potential for escalating violence and/or severe repression which the urban rioting and the subsequent white backlash presented.

The Black Panthers

Another organization dedicated to a form of Black Power emerged on the West Coast in 1966. Huey Newton and Bobby Seale, working within what they believed to be the tradition and spirit of Malcolm X but also drawing on the ideas of other Black organizations that had emphasized the need for self-defense, formed the Black Panther Party in Oakland, California. Shortly thereafter, Eldridge Cleaver, also an admirer of Malcolm X, just out of prison and author of a widely acclaimed book, *Soul On Ice,* joined the Black Panthers as Minister of Information. Cleaver's major responsibility was to edit the Party's newspaper, *The Black Panther.*[54] The initial purpose of the organization was to confront the problem of police brutality in the Black community of Oakland. Like all other relatively successful Black organizations, the Panthers were keenly aware of symbols and ideological codes in developing their tactics. With particular attention to the letter of the law, the Panthers made it their policy to carry weapons for the purpose of self-defense. The right to bear arms for self-defense is an individual right protected by the Constitution.

In the beginning, the Panthers' major program involved conducting police patrols. Members of the Panther organization would carry guns and follow police cars on their rounds. Wherever the police made an arrest, the Panthers would observe the arrest and sometimes read aloud from a law book the legal rights of the offender. In their contact with the police, the Panthers used abusive (not profane as that would be grounds for arrest) language. In general, they demonstrated defiance when confronting armed police in a way that clearly was psychologically satisfying and symbolically important to the self-identity and self-pride of many of those previously intimidated by the police.[55] The white police were the most immediate physical and symbolic token of white oppression for many in the Black community. To have Black men willing to risk death by defying such white symbols was extremely important, particularly to many Black ghetto youth.

The program of self-defense brought a particularly intense and one-dimensional reaction from many in the white community. The image of angry young Blacks carrying guns was an electrifying symbol to whites, one that brought media attention to the group. Self-defense, however, was not the only aspect of the Panther program. Other ideas of Malcolm X were also present. Primary among these was a stated distrust of the United States government. The Panthers believed that the government was an enemy, "the agency of a ruling clique that controls the country."[56] In viewing other Black self-defense organizations such as Robert Williams's organization in Monroe, N.C. (which was originally connected with the NAACP and a Black chapter of the National Rifle Association) or the Deacons for Defense and Justice in Louisiana, Newton and Seale did not want to emulate the way those organizations relied on the federal government for assistance. While the Panthers sought housing, jobs, food, education, justice, and peace as did the nonviolent civil-rights groups, they made it clear that if these demands were not met, then the means of production should be taken from the businessmen and "placed in the hands of the community." If white landlords continued to deny decent housing to Blacks, housing and land should be made into cooperatives controlled by the community. Since Black people had been put in prison by white juries, all prisoners should be released and courts should be reformed to ensure trial by one's peers. With regard to education, the Panthers did not demand equal education but rather "education that exposes the true nature of this decadent American Society. We want education that teaches us our true history and our role in the present-day society."[57]

While the program of the Panthers evolved as both Blacks and whites responded to its message of self-defense for Black people, the Black Panther Party's message throughout this period is a fascinating synthesis of ideological themes and actions drawn from both the separatist and the integrationist movements in Black history. By 1966, the nonviolent civil-rights movement clearly was losing its appeal in the Black community. The movement had grown well beyond the Southern Christian Church constituency that had provided the core of Martin Luther King's Black following. The Old Testament, the songs of slavery, the nonviolent workshops, were not enough in the face of continued bombings, police brutality, and token compromises such as the Civil Rights Acts of 1964 and even 1965. These acts had promised basic improvements in the quality of life for Black people through the electoral system (a questionable premise in and of itself); but then enforcement of even those presumed "gains" was denied.

Martin Luther King's nonviolent tactics did very little for Black identity and Black pride, especially in Northern urban ghettos. King's strategy required that Blacks accept more degradation, more punishment, more repression of their own dignity as the mechanism for changing the law. The Panthers' self-defense message clearly countered that particular problem of the nonviolent campaign and addressed itself primarily to developing self-identity in the Black community. To wear guns and advocate self-defense was a tactic that attracted young Blacks. To the extent that the Black Panthers were successful in standing up to the police, they won the admiration of others in the community. King had warned Carmichael and McKissick when they used Black Power as a vague slogan in Mississippi in 1966 that the nonviolent rhetoric and tactic was the only way to agitate for improvements and still avoid mass bloodshed and a heightened repression of the Black community. The white majority's capacity for violence far surpassed anything a Black community might possibly develop.

In a sense, the Panthers' police patrols were an attempt to apply the civil-rights tactics without the nonviolence rhetoric. Just as King appealed to the United States Constitution and the concept of equal protection of the laws, the Panthers sought protection in the Constitutional right to bear arms. The patrols carried law books and were extremely careful to comply with all traffic and vehicle codes. Martin Luther King's nonviolent campaign strategy was to develop "creative tension" as a bargaining tactic for obtaining specific concessions that would improve the lives of Black people in a particular community. The Panthers' patrols also created tension, specifically in the Oakland police force. Unlike King, the Panthers were not interested in verbal bargaining with the police. At best, they expected to reduce police brutality in the Black community in Oakland while helping to build community pride and identity for waging revolution (or future battles). At the worst, Black Panthers expected to be killed by the police and thereby to provide a symbol of Black resistance to an oppressive white government.

Another interesting comparison between the Panthers' tactics and those of the nonviolent civil-rights movement concerns the way each

3. The Minority Politics of Black America

group worked to obtain media coverage of its activities and its message to attract both white and Black allies. White reaction to the Panthers' police patrols created the opportunity for the Panthers to attract national media coverage that otherwise would never have been available. As a direct response to the Panthers' activities, a Republican state Assemblyman from Oakland, Don Mulford, introduced a bill that forbade the carrying of loaded weapons within incorporated areas. In reply, on May 2, 1967, the Panthers sent 23 men, most of them armed, and 6 women to Sacramento to "lobby" against the bill and to read a statement to the media. The statement condemned the United States government for its participation in the Vietnam war, for its history of enslavement and brutality exercised against Black people, American Indians, and Japanese Americans. The statement noted that Black people had begged, prayed, petitioned, and demonstrated to no avail and it called on Black people to arm themselves against the terror of police brutality and repression "before it is too late."[58] The newsworthy event of the "lobbying" tactic, of course, was not the statement but rather the fact that the members of the lobbying delegation were wearing or carrying weapons into the Capitol. This was the message that the media carried to both whites and Blacks around the country. Although the legislature passed the Mulford bill in July 1967 and thereby ended the Panthers' police patrols, the "lobbying" effort had triggered considerable positive response from Blacks across the nation and marked the establishment of the Black Panthers as a national organization with chapters in every major United States city. Antiwar protesters, Students for a Democratic Society, the Weathermen, and many other lesser-known groups also responded positively to the Black Panthers' militant stand.

With the police patrols no longer possible, the Panthers' program focused on other issues. One problem was the arrest of Panther leaders. In October 1967, the Oakland police stopped Huey Newton in a car at night. A confrontation ensued which left Newton wounded, one policeman wounded, and another policeman dead. Newton went to jail to await trial. The Black Panthers used his arrest to mobilize a "Free Huey" campaign which emphasized the idea that Huey Newton could not possibly obtain a fair trial under the racist circumstances that governed the courts and juries. Neither the grand jury nor the trial jury had Black representation proportional to the Black population of Alameda County. After a series of trials and appeals, Newton was released from prison in August 1970 and finally acquitted of charges in 1971.[59]

In April 1968, Eldridge Cleaver was arrested for violation of parole. Rather than return to prison, Cleaver chose to leave the country. First he went to Cuba and then to Algeria. Bobby Seale was charged in April

1969, along with seven others, with conspiring to incite a riot at the Chicago Democratic Convention in 1968 and again charged in May 1969 with murder and conspiracy to commit murder in the killing of Black Panther Alex Rackley in Connecticut. Seale was convicted of contempt of court, but the murder charges were finally dismissed in May 1971.[60] In July 1971, David Hilliard, who had kept the Party together after the arrests of Newton, Seale, and Cleaver, was sent to prison for one to ten years for assaulting a police officer with a deadly weapon in April 1968. Similar arrests of other Black Panthers occurred throughout this period. The House Committee on Internal Security reported that 348 Panthers were jailed in 1969.[61] On December 4, 1969, Chicago police raided Panther headquarters, killing two Panthers, Fred Hampton and Mark Clark, and wounding four others. The federal grand jury later concluded that the policemen's claim to have fired in self-defense was false.[62] While the Panthers knew that the FBI and other police enforcement agencies had declared war on their organization, the general public became aware of the extent of this vendetta only with the Watergate episode and the opening of FBI files in the 1970s. The Panthers' "Free Huey" campaign consequently was the beginning of a number of consciousness-raising drives aimed at exposing the biases and conditions that prevailed in the courts and in the prisons of the country. The Panthers established their first prison chapter in February 1971 at San Quentin Prison in California to support and publicize the cases of George Jackson and the Soledad Brothers as well as of seven Chicanos awaiting trial in San Francisco for killing a police officer.

A second strategy of the Black Panthers in 1968 involved allying themselves with white antiwar groups and with other minority groups for mutual benefit. In March 1968, the Panthers met with some of these other groups to form the mostly white Peace and Freedom Party for the purpose of running candidates for election in 1968. This tactic provided a platform and media coverage for the revolutionary messages that the Panthers and various other antiwar groups sought to convey. As a candidate for President, Eldridge Cleaver reiterated many of Malcolm X's themes, saying that Black people in the United States are colonialized and that they need to establish "political and military machinery" to effect both a revolution in the "white mother country" and "national liberation for the Black colony."[63] In other attempts at coalition building the Panthers unsuccessfully explored the possibility of merging with SNCC in 1968. In 1969, they did form an official alliance with the Students for a Democratic Society.

After Newton had been jailed and Cleaver had fled the country in 1968, Seale led the Black Panthers in expanding and implementing the

3. The Minority Politics of Black America   53

"Serve the People" program, which involved free breakfasts for children, free health clinics, Black-liberation schools, and community control of urban police. Of these, the free-breakfast program was the most successful. By 1970, the Panther organization was well established in over 30 cities of the nation. The Panthers' weekly newsletter had a circulation of almost 10,000 and at 25 cents a copy provided most of the revenue for operating the organization. In ideology, the Panthers shifted more and more toward the language of Marxism-Leninism as they allied with white groups and sought connections with national-liberation movements outside of the United States.

The Black Panther Party, however, was plagued by internal dissension and demoralized by the continuing toll inflicted on Panther members by police raids, arrests, trials, and prison sentences. By late 1971, Huey Newton admitted that "the Party was very wrong to think that it could change the police forces in the way we tried to do it. All we got was a war and a lot of bloodshed."[64] The Party had in its political activities moved away from the Black community. To become more effective, Newton argued, the Party had to return to the community and listen to the desires and needs of Black people. Throughout the 1970s, the Black Panthers continued to work for reform of the courts, juries, and prisons. They continued to speak out against police brutality and mounted campaigns against the Bakke and Watson cases which tested "reverse discrimination" in admission programs and in job opportunities. The Panthers also expanded their interest in international liberation movements in Africa, Asia, and Latin America. A sympathetic concern with the antinuclear movement was also a part of the Panther program in the late 1970s.[65]

Black Studies—Pan-African Movements

In 1968, the Afro-American Student Organizations on various campuses across the country began to demand that colleges and universities not only admit more Black and other minority students, but also develop curricula that did not cater to the European bias that pervades education in the United States. The Panthers, SNCC, Students for a Democratic Society, and a variety of other organizations joined the Black students in demanding courses on Black culture, Black literature, and especially Black history. These students also demanded Black Studies or Afro-American Studies departments with Black faculty and Black autonomy over hiring and firing.[66] In April 1968, students at Columbia University occupied five university buildings and staged a sit-in for a week. They also held two administrators captive for a short while as a means of developing bargaining power for their demands. One of these demands involved stopping construction on a school gymnasium scheduled to occupy one of the few urban parks in Harlem; another demanded that the University sever its ties with the Institute for Defense Analysis.

Similar protests and demonstrations occurred at colleges and universities across the nation. At San Francisco State College, students struck in November 1968 to demand the establishment of a Black Studies Department. The immediate issue for mobilizing this strike was the firing of Black Panther George Murray. The idea of a Black Studies Department had been under consideration at the school for over a year. Dr. Nathan Hare had been hired from Howard University to develop the curriculum. During the fall of 1968, the board of trustees was having difficulty agreeing to institute the program. The student strike provided the catalyst. The board finally accepted a program by the end of the year which included a separate and autonomous Black Studies program.

At some schools, such as Yale University, changing the curriculum to incorporate the Black experience did not require protests and demonstrations. By holding a Black Studies conference at Yale in early 1968, the Black students were able to convince enough faculty and administrators that such a curriculum change was desirable. Yale responded not by creating a separate Black Studies Department but by establishing a degree-granting program in Afro-American Studies composed of forty-five existing courses that related to the Afro-American experience. An interdisciplinary faculty committee whose members held positions in already established departments administered the program. Yale and San Francisco State became the model programs for Black Studies around the country.[67]

What was clear in the Black Studies movement that swept across the campuses of the nation in 1968, 1969, and into 1970 was the fact that militancy on the part of Black students could bring results. Most Black Student Unions and Afro-American Student Organizations had a core of militant leaders who decided strategy, tactics, programs, and general policy. While the Black Panthers did not dominate these organizations, members of the Panther Party often participated. The immediate stated goal of the Black Studies movement was ideological. In practice, money and jobs were also involved, as the budgets for Black Studies departments were not inconsiderable. The two strongest ideological trends in the Black Studies Movement were Black cultural nationalism and what might be called a neo-Marxist international ideological position that encouraged Black people to analyze their situation in global economic terms and to identify with oppressed and colonialized people everywhere. Conflict between these two positions occurred in the establishment of Black Studies programs in a number of instances.[68]

The International Orientation of Black Politics during the 1970s

During the 1970s, Black political leaders moved to solidify and administer the gains won by the militants of the 1960s. They also continued to turn their attention toward global affairs. This was not a new development. Many Black political groups have sought to transcend national boundaries. W. E. B. Dubois participated in Pan African Congresses throughout the first two decades of the century, pressing for independence for African nations and Black people in general. Garvey's Universal Negro Improvement Association was itself international, with branches in the Caribbean, Latin America, and Africa. Racial unity was one of its major goals. Blacks in the United States identified with Ethiopia in 1935 and some even went to fight with the Ethiopians against fascist Italy. Martin Luther King, Jr., carefully studied and emulated the nonviolent tactics of Mahatma Gandhi in India's independence movement against the British. India gained independence just seven years before King founded the Southern Christian Leadership Conference. Many American Blacks observed with intense interest the various independence movements of African nations during the 1950s and 1960s and celebrated each victory. However, choosing sides in African politics became much more difficult during the postindependence struggles that developed within these new nations. The civil war in Nigeria and the various conflicting Black independence movements in Zimbabwe and Angola generated confusion among American Blacks. Of course, South Africa with its apartheid policies was and continues to be a rallying point.

While interest in and concern with foreign affairs has long standing in the United States Black community, the success of the civil-rights movement in the late 1960s and the increased electoral power of Blacks in the 1970s turned Black interest towards United States foreign policy. Martin Luther King's opposition to the Vietnam war was a beginning. Increasingly, United States Black organizations developed linkages with foreign groups or nations outside Africa. Malcolm X and Muhammad Ali directed the attention of American Blacks towards the Islamic and Arab worlds. The Black Panthers developed linkages with the Palestine

Liberation Organization. In 1971, Libya gave $3 million to the Black Muslims.[69] President Carter's appointment of long-time civil-rights campaigner Andrew Young to be United States Ambassador to the United Nations was particularly significant. Young's personal mission while at the United Nations was to direct United States attention to the concerns of developing nations. This personal commitment was backed by the economic reality of growing United States trade with developing countries. In 1978, developing nations were responsible for 46 percent of all United States overseas sales ($53 billion). Oil-exporting countries were responsible for only about a third of these sales ($16 billion). Of all United States imports, developing countries contributed 42 percent of the total. Oil-producing countries accounted for about half of this figure.[70]

For some members of the Black community in the United States, the increased attention of the nation to less-developed nations offered an opportunity for the Black movement to recapture the spark of the 1960s and to attract media attention to the cause. The Reverend Joseph Lowery, head of the Southern Christian Leadership Conference, made a tour of Guyana after the Jonestown suicides and also went on a well-publicized visit to Beirut with Jesse Jackson, leader of PUSH, to preach nonviolence to Yasser Arafat of the Palestine Liberation Organization (PLO). When Andrew Young was forced to resign from his United Nations post in 1979 because of his meeting with a Palestine Liberation Organization official in violation of an official United States policy not to deal with the PLO, Lowery along with other leaders of the Southern Christian Leadership Conference met with Palestinian diplomats and declared their support for "the human rights of all Palestinians," including the right of self-determination in regard to their own homeland. The Americans also met with Israeli officials. Later, in response to criticism, Lowery declared that the Southern Christian Leadership Conference had not supported terrorism by making its statement about Palestinian rights.[71]

Ideological Assessments of Black Politics

Lockean Liberals and Pragmatic Utilitarians are of several minds in their evaluation of Black politics during the last thirty years. Lockean Liberals support the principle of equal treatment and individual rights; however, they oppose programs that provide preferential treatment for Blacks or that establish quotas. The Lockean Liberal would reward individual achievement and would allow Blacks to hold whatever jobs they individually can perform and to live wherever they choose and can afford to live. However, positive programs such as encouraging Black people to move into white suburbs or providing special educational opportunities for Blacks are an anathema.

Pragmatic Utilitarians, in contrast, point to the electoral gains and the new opportunities for education and jobs that positive governmental programs made available in the 1970s for Blacks. By February 1970, 47 Black mayors had been elected to office, many in large urban areas such as Cleveland, Gary, and Newark.[72] Numerous other Blacks had been elected to local and state positions. In Washington in 1971, the thirteen Black members of the House of Representatives formed the Congressional Black Caucus to promote Black interests and to publicize disagreements with the Nixon Administration. This group has continued to operate. Pragmatic Utilitarians also note that the recessions of 1969 to 1971 and 1973 to 1975 hit Black workers the hardest, especially those who were not college graduates or white-collar workers, or did not have seniority on the job. The institutional patterns of job discrimination that have existed for many years remain in force. The recessions and the resulting unemployment are creating a growing gap within the Black community between those who have some degree of job security and those who do not. The Pragmatic Utilitarian solution to this problem is to develop more programs that will target the needs of the "underclass" to attempt to keep it from becoming hopelessly submerged. The idea of quotas and preferential treatment has a much stronger legitimacy for Pragmatic Utilitarians than it has for Lockean Liberals because of the Pragmatic Utilitarian's emphasis on the importance of representation for all interests.

Those critical of both the Lockean Liberal and the Pragmatic Utilitarian positions evaluate the civil-rights movement as having gained symbolic victories while in reality keeping Black people as impoverished and impotent as ever. Piven and Cloward argue that the United States government in the late 1960s successfully diverted the militancy generated by the civil-rights and Black Power movements into electoral gains for Blacks and into socioeconomic programs such as the War on Poverty, the Elementary and Secondary Education Act, and the Model Cities programs. In addition, private institutions such as universities and corporations began admitting or hiring Black people in somewhat greater numbers. The problem, they argue, is that Black people have been divided and engulfed by bureaucratic and political institutions that dissipate the energies of the movement as a whole, while compelling dissent to be focused in small cliques or caucuses that attempt to exert Black Power on issues that do not mobilize mass constituencies.

Certainly it is true that Black people in the 1980s are no longer segregated from whites in the use of public facilities as they were in 1960.

Also, many Black people have been able to move into public and private jobs that were previously closed. However, the material wealth and the life chances of Black people have not changed significantly. Black youth continue to have a much higher unemployment rate than white youth, just as Black adults as a whole continue to have a higher unemployment rate in comparison with whites. The economic status of Blacks relative to whites is worse than it was ten years ago.[73] Prisons continue to have over 40 percent of their populations composed either of Blacks or of other nonwhite minorities, when these minorities constitute only about 12 percent of the total population.[74]

One of the central arguments of this book is that while material gains have been slim, the ideological contribution that the history and political tactics of Blacks in the United States have offered the nation as a whole must not be dismissed. The political and psychological struggles of Black people in opposing their own designation as an "other" by the dominant ideological positions in the society have contributed significantly to changing the consciousness of the United States public. The political activities of Blacks have changed the image and identity of both Black and white people and have shattered many ideological expectations concerning government. The contradictions are now on display. For those who have learned that genuine political and social change requires far-reaching changes in social interactions, consciousness, and values as well as changes in economic and political institutions, the contributions of Black politics in the United States have been enormous. To measure success only in terms of changes in material wealth or political power for a particular group is to ignore the extent to which symbols, ideology, and values contribute to the nature and quality of a society. The struggle of Black people, originally defined as property in a Lockean Liberal legal system, has been and continues to be a remarkable process of political education for the nation.

Notes For Chapter 3

1. Letter from James Forten to Paul Cuffe; 25 January 1817, in *Black Nationalism in America*, ed. John H. Bracey, Jr., August Meier, and Elliott Rudwick (Indianapolis: Bobbs-Merrill, 1970), pp. 45–46.

2. For a discussion of this trend see John Hope Franklin, *From Slavery to Freedom: A History of Negro Americans*, 3rd ed. (New York: Knopf, 1967), pp. 433–439. Also see Lerone Bennett, *Confrontation in Black and White* (Baltimore: Penguin Books, 1965), pp. 72–77.

3. The Minority Politics of Black America

3. Booker T. Washington, "The Atlanta Exposition Address, September, 1895," in August Meier, Elliott Rudwick, and Francis L. Broderick, ed., *Black Protest Thought in the Twentieth Century* (Indianapolis: Bobbs-Merrill, 1971), pp. 3–8.

4. See W. E. B. Dubois, "To the Nations of the World," leaflet, 1900, in Meier, Rudwick, and Broderick, pp. xxvii, 55–58. See also Bracey, Meier, and Rudwick, pp. 246–262; 269–278 (note 1 above).

5. For more on Garvey see: Amy Jacques Garvey, ed., *Philosophy and Opinions of Marcus Garvey* (New York: Atheneum, 1969); E. David Cronon, *Black Moses: The Story of Marcus Garvey and the Universal Negro Improvement Association* (Madison: University of Wisconsin Press, 1969). Amy Jacques Garvey, *Garvey and Garveyism* (Kingston, Jamaica: A. Jacques Garvey, 1963). Adolph Edwards, *Marcus Garvey, 1887–1940*, London, New Beacon Publication, 1967).

6. Marcus Garvey, "Speech on Disarmament," delivered at Liberty Hall, New York, 6 November 1921, in Garvey, *Philosophy and Opinions*, p. 111 (note 5 above).

7. Marcus Garvey, "Speech on Disarmament."

8. Marcus Garvey, "The Image of God," in Garvey, *Philosophy and Opinions*, p. 44.

9. For a short summary of Garvey's life see: Hollis R. Lynch. "Introduction to the Atheneum Edition" in Garvey, *Philosophy and Opinions*. Also see Franklin, pp. 490–493 (note 2 above).

10. C. Eric Lincoln. *The Black Muslims in America* (Boston: Beacon, 1961), pp. 76–77. See also Bracey, Meier, and Rudwick, pp. 403–427 (note 1 above).

11. See E. U. Essien-Udom, *Black Nationalism: A Search for Identity in America* (Chicago: University of Chicago Press, 1962).

12. Malcolm X, with the assistance of Alex Haley, *The Autobiography of Malcolm X* (New York: Grove Press, 1964). George Breitman, *The Last Year of Malcolm X: The Evolution of a Revolutionary* (New York: Merit Publishers, 1967).

13. Malcolm X, p. 371.

14. Malcolm X, p. 375.

15. Booker T. Washington, "The Atlanta Exposition Address," pp. 3–8 in Meier, Rudwick, and Broderick (note 3 above). For more on Washington's philosophy, see pp. 8–18. Also see Washington, *Up from Slavery* (New York: Doubleday, 1901).

16. For more on W. E. B. Dubois, the Niagara movement, and the NAACP, see Meier, Rudwick, and Broderick, pp. 47–55, 58–60 (note 3 above).

17. For an excellent account of this effort, see Richard Kluger, *Simple Justice: A History of Brown v. Board of Education and America's Struggle for Equality* (New York: Vintage, 1977).

18. *Guinn v. United States*, 238 U.S. 347 (1915).

19. *Buchanan v. Warley*, 245 U.S. 60 (1917).

20. *Moore v. Dempsey*, 261 U.S. 86 (1923).

21. *Alston v. School Board of Norfolk*, 12 F. 2d 992 (1940), cert. denied 311 U.S. 693 (1940).

22. *Henderson v. United States*, 339 U.S. 816 (1950).

23. *Smith v. Allwright*, 321 U.S. 649 (1944).

24. Louis E. Lomax, *The Negro Revolt* (New York: Signet, 1963), pp. 122–123.

25. Frances Fox Piven and Richard A. Cloward, *Poor People's Movements: Why They Succeed, How They Fail* (New York: Pantheon, 1977), pp. 189–194.

26. Lomax, p. 119.

27. Robert Allen, *Black Awakening in Capitalist America* (New York: Doubleday, 1969), pp. 102–103.

28. Lomax, p. 119.

29. Franklin, pp. 578–579 (note 2 above).

30. Lomax, p. 145.

31. Lomax, p. 134.

32. Lomax, p. 104–105.

33. Lomax, p. 104–105.

34. For an account of the Freedom Ride Movement, see Lomax, pp. 144–159.

35. Martin Luther King, Jr., "Letter from Birmingham Jail," in *Why We Can't Wait* (New York: Harper and Row, 1963), pp. 77–100.

36. King.

37. Michael Lipsky, "Protest as a Political Resource," *American Political Science Review* 62 (March 1968): 1144–1158.

38. William A. Gamson, *The Strategy of Social Protest* (Homewood, Ill.: Dorsey, 1975).

39. Bennett, pp. 239–240 (note 2 above).

40. Piven and Cloward, p. 225 (note 25 above).

3. The Minority Politics of Black America

41. Theodore White, *The Making of the President, 1960* (New York: Atheneum, 1961). Theodore Sorensen, *Kennedy* (New York: Harper, 1965). Arthur M. Schlesinger, Jr., *A Thousand Days* (Boston: Houghton Mifflin, 1965).

42. Piven and Cloward, p. 228 (note 25 above).

43. For an excellent account of events during this period, see Piven and Cloward, pp. 248-255 (note 25 above).

44. Piven and Cloward, p. 251 (note 25 above).

45. Martin Luther King, Jr., *Where Do We Go From Here? Chaos or Community* (Boston: Beacon, 1967), pp. 32-44.

46. King, *Where*, p. 47.

47. King, *Where*, p. 45.

48. King, *Where*, p. 57.

49. King, *Where*, p. 57.

50. Stokely Carmichael and Charles V. Hamilton, *Black Power: The Politics of Liberation in America* (New York: Random House, 1967).

51. Allen, p. 30 (note 27 above).

52. Breitman, p. 33 (note 12 above).

53. Carmichael and Hamilton (note 50 above).

54. Huey P. Newton, *Revolutionary Suicide* (New York: Ballantine, 1973), pp. 149-150.

55. Newton, pp. 127-142.

56. Newton, p. 125.

57. Newton, p. 130.

58. Newton, pp. 162-168.

59. Newton, p. 329.

60. Newton, pp. 328-329.

61. U.S. Congress, House, Committee on Internal Security, *Hearings*, 92nd Congress, 1st Session, 18 August 1971, as reported by Robert Brisbane, *Black Activism* (Valley Forge, Pa.: Judson Press, 1974), p. 219.

62. Philip S. Foner, ed., *The Black Panthers Speak* (New York: Lippincott, 1970), p. 137.

63. Eldridge Cleaver, "Speech Given at the Founding of the Peace and Freedom Party," reported in Allen, p. 264 (note 27 above).

64. "Newton Concedes Panther Errors," *Washington Post,* 21 May 1971, Sec. A, p. 3.

65. See issues of *The Black Panther,* a weekly publication (Oakland, California, 1979).

66. For a discussion of Black Studies programs, see Brisbane, pp. 223-244 (note 61 above). Nathan Hare, "What Should Be the Role of Afro-American Education in the Undergraduate Curriculum," *Liberal Education* 55 (March 1969): 42-50. Nick Aron Ford, *Black Studies: Threat of Challenge* (Port Washington, N.Y.: Kennikat Press, 1973), pp. 105-135.

67. Brisbane, pp. 229-230 (note 61 above).

68. Perhaps the most visible of these disputes erupted at the University of California, Los Angeles, in January 1969, when a conflict developed between Ron Karenga's Los Angeles-based cultural nationalist organization US and the Black Panthers over the directorship of the Afro-American Studies Center that had just been established. At a meeting on the UCLA campus between the two groups concerning the matter, two Black Panthers were shot and killed. Usually, however, the ideological and political wrangling did not result in such a tragic end. See Newton, p. 284, for a Panther view of the affair (note 54 above).

69. Brisbane, p. 258 (note 61 above).

70. Piven and Cloward, pp. 254-255 (note 25 above).

71. Pranay B. Gupte, "Israeli at UN Meets with Blacks and Criticizes Support of PLO," *New York Times,* 26 August, 1979, Sec. A, p. 4. See also "10 Blacks from U.S. Tour South Lebanon, Meet with Guerrillas," *New York Times,* 20 September, 1979, Sec. A, p. 3.

72. Piven and Cloward, p. 255 (note 25 above).

73. Black youth unemployment in 1977 was 25 percent, white youth unemployment 13.7 percent. Black unemployment in general was 13 percent in 1977, white unemployment 6.2 percent. Black median income in 1959 was $5000. By 1974, it had risen to $8000. White median income in 1959 was $10,000. By 1974, it had risen to $13,000. In education, Blacks have made some gains. In 1970, 52 percent of the Black population had completed four years of high school; only 6 percent of Blacks had completed four years of college. In 1975, 69 percent of Blacks had completed high school and 11 percent had finished college. Whites completing high school increased from 74 percent to 82 percent between 1970 and 1975. Whites completing college increased from 17 percent to 22 percent. See U.S. Bureau of the Census, *The Social and Economic Status of the Black Population in the United States: An Historical View,* Current Population Reports, Special Series P-23, No. 80 (Washington, D.C.: U.S. Department of Commerce) pp. 22, 59, 85. See also U.S. Bureau of the Census, *Statistical Abstract of the United States,* 100th ed. (Washington, D.C.: U.S. Government Printing Office, 1979).

74. Of the 26,193 persons in federal prisons in 1977, 10,309 (39 percent) were nonwhites. Of the 141,600 persons in jail in 1977, 58,900 (41.6 percent) were nonwhites. U.S. Bureau of the Census, *Statistical Abstract of the United States, 1978* (Washington, D.C.: U.S. Government Printing Office, 1978), p. 200.

Chapter 4

The Minority Politics of Women

The strategic position of women in American society is unique in comparison with other minority groups, in that women have been more completely absorbed psychologically and physically into the political and economic struggles of male-dominated institutions and factions. Women, consequently, have a much more difficult job of establishing their own identity and unity as women than have other minority groups. This close integration of women into the dominant institutions of the society makes any attempt on the part of women to break out of traditional arrangements especially challenging and revolutionary with regard to the dominant order. Through institutions such as marriage and the family, women and men relate to one another in prescribed and coded patterns that are articulated, formalized, and reinforced by religious, political, and economic institutions. When women begin to question their prescribed role in the society, they are strategically in a position to challenge in fundamental ways the operations of practically all institutions in the society. Whereas Blacks in the United States constitute only about 12 percent of the total population and have been confined historically to segregated education and housing arrangements, women constitute over half of the population and in life style and social status occupy all levels and classes in the society. Many whites in American society have no close association with Blacks. Practically all men, on the other hand, have a close emotional tie to at least one woman. This strategic situation of women constitutes both the strength and the weakness of women in United States politics.

A Brief History

As with all minority movements, women's liberation struggles have been the most active during times of economic instability and change. Historically, the women's movement has followed the lead of Black liberation struggles in the United States. From the beginning, the women's movement has been composed primarily of upper- and middle-class educated white women. The first women's-rights movement emerged out of the abolitionist movement just prior to the Civil War and finally reached its climax in the passage of the Nineteenth Amendment to the Constitution, which gave women the vote in 1920. From 1920 to 1960, the militancy of the women's movement declined.

Instead of uniting politically as a group, women increasingly joined existing political movements that dealt more with economic than with sexual issues.[1] Some of the early suffrage leaders, such as Susan B. Anthony, had expected that granting women the vote would revolutionize society. Others, like Elizabeth Cady Stanton, had been more skeptical, arguing that the position of women in society was too deeply rooted in religious and political ideologies and practices to expect that granting women the vote would alone radically change the status of women or the nature of the society. When women finally did obtain the vote, a women's voting bloc did not materialize. No issue clearly divided the sexes. Many women were politically active, promoting and working for New Deal issues involving government provision of social services; they took part in the CIO labor movement and worked in the Socialist and Communist Parties. However, many more women were supporting traditional women's roles in society.

During World War II, many of the social forces that created the conditions for the Black civil-rights movement in the 1950s and 1960s were also affecting women. Between 1940 and 1945, women joined the labor force in large numbers. Jobs opened in many areas previously reserved for men. By 1945, 50 percent more women were working than were in 1940, the membership of women in unions had quadrupled, and women as a group were earning considerably more money.[2] However, after the war, many women left the work force and returned to the home. The articulation of women's issues as such did not occur until the 1960s, after many middle-class white women had identified with and learned from the civil-rights and the Black Power movements.

During the early 1960s, the civil-rights movement, the sit-ins, the freedom rides, and the boycotts occupied national attention and the national media. Many young white women active in the Free Speech Movement, the Student Nonviolent Coordinating Committee (SNCC), the Students for a Democratic Society (SDS), and in various antiwar protest organizations found themselves not only embroiled in the politics of protest but also very cognizant of the fact that second-class status in American society defined not only Black and Brown people but women also. By learning to understand the psychic and political problems of Black people, women came to realize their own psychic imprisonment within traditional institutions and ideologies.

This awakening took place on a number of different levels and was implemented by a number of factors. In 1960, oral contraceptives first became widely available. These ushered in a whole new era in sexual freedom for women, who previously had often had to bear such burdensome consequences of sexual intercourse as unwanted childbirth or illegal abortion. For many women, having a sure means of avoiding pregnancy other than sexual abstinence was enormously liberating psychologically.

In 1963, Betty Friedan published her book, *The Feminine Mystique,* which outlined in explicit detail the socialization process and social structure that directed middle-class women into the psychologically debilitating role of full-time housewife. The book hit a very sensitive public nerve as it became an immediate best seller.

Also in 1963, Congress finally passed the Equal Pay Act, which provided that women receive the same pay as men doing the same jobs. This bill had been first introduced in 1945. In a parliamentary move, women were able to persuade Congress to include women in Title VII of the Civil Rights Act of 1964.[3] This section required equal employment opportunity for Black men and for Black and white women. The act established the Equal Employment Opportunity Commission to administer the bill. Women generally found, however, that the Equal Employment Opportunity Commission was not taking Title VII seriously with regard to their treatment. To pressure the government to implement the law, women organized the National Organization for Women (NOW) in 1966, and by 1967 had developed a series of demands. These included the Equal Rights Amendment, the enforcement of laws prohibiting sex discrimination in employment, the establishment of child-care centers, tax deductions for child care, maternity leave, rights in employment, Social Security rights, and the right of women to control their own reproductive lives, especially with regard to legalized abortions.[4]

A radical element began to emerge during this period. Many women had their first political experience. They entered the civil-rights campaign with Pragmatic Utilitarian ideas, expecting their political activity to bring significant observable changes. As the Black Power and the antiwar movements became discouraged by the failure of protest tactics to implement any material change, many women began to question their Pragmatic Utilitarian ideas. By 1965, it was clear that New Left organizations —such as the Student Nonviolent Coordinating Committee and Students for a Democratic Society—had no sympathy for women's issues. While dedicated to changing society totally, these groups continued to treat women as second-class citizens. Outraged by having their issues ignored or rejected at a 1965 SDS conference, small groups of women began meeting in Chicago, New York, and Maryland to engage in consciousness raising and to take specific stands on issues such as abortion.[5] The same kind of consciousness raising was also occurring in England. These women began to realize that changing the status of women would involve psychological and institutional changes penetrating all institutions in society. Since the oppression of women existed prior to any existing economic or social order, many women have come to understand that changing economic relationships, while important, will not necessarily bring about any particular change in sex roles. Maintaining the male orientation and domination of Western society involved other factors that needed to be identified and addressed.

The most interesting and the most politically significant aspect of the women's movement is the challenge it presents to the Pragmatic Utilitarian ideology which gives it legitimacy. The Pragmatic Utilitarian ideology holds that all interests in the society ought to have a voice in decision-making and thereby legitimates the participation of women in governmental decision-making. The Pragmatic Utilitarian ideology also argues that there is a distinction between what is public and what is private. Public decisions are those whose consequences affect more than those involved in making the decision. Both the Lockean Liberal and Pragmatic Utilitarian ideologies have traditionally viewed women's issues as being in the private sphere. The Lockean Liberal view is one that would clearly define women's issues as ungermane to the business of government. The Pragmatic Utilitarian is willing to expand the public sphere in accordance with established procedures.

The dilemma that develops here is that women's issues penetrate practically every every aspect of society, thereby obliterating the traditional distinctions between the public and private. The very process of bringing sex and gender questions out of the unconscious and into the political arena for debate and rationalization dramatically illustrates that there is no private sphere. For women, unconscious attitudes and acts have public consequences. The women's movement inevitably raises the point that an ideology is not just a rational set of ideas and formal relationships but that it is rather a reflection of interpersonal relationships and habits that exist at unarticulated and often unconscious levels of thought. The private is not private at all but is an integral part of the total social order.

Consequently, evaluations of the political successes or failures of the movement cannot be confined to noting changes in the economic or legal status of women, although these changes are certainly a vital part of the process. What is clear in both the feminist and the antifeminist arguments is that some articulated explanation is needed to account for the status of women. The political thrust of the women's movement is primarily ideological and psychological in that it raises sex-gender issues from the level of unexamined custom to the level of public policy in a variety of different ways. In discussing and describing the women's movement, this chapter will review the main assumptions and activities of the Pragmatic Utilitarian, the Antifeminist, the Radical Feminist, and the Socialist Feminist positions. Since the Pragmatic Utilitarian ideology has motivated many aspects of the women's movement, it is appropriate to discuss the Pragmatic Feminist position and the political strategies it inspires before turning to the others.

The Pragmatic Feminist Position

The Pragmatic Feminist view is based on the individual's natural right to self-preservation and the pursuit of happiness. For the Pragmatic Feminist, men and women are not biologically or morally different in their right to self-preservation or in their ability to decide what brings happiness and what brings pain. Sexual inequality on this fundamental issue does not exist. The observed status difference between men and women in society consequently is social and political in origin, not biological or religious.

The Pragmatic Feminist position has a clear concept of public and private within it. Within the public sphere, all individuals have a natural right to equal opportunity and equal treatment. Within the private sphere, individuals are and should be different and consequently unequal. The public is differentiated from the private by virtue of the consequences of various acts. A private act will have consequences that affect only those who participate. A public act, in contrast, is any act whose consequences affect others who do not participate. The private sphere becomes public as individuals come together to realize that certain acts previously defined as private are affecting them as a group and not solely as individuals.

Women began coming together to identify women's issues as the concern of the public in 1848. At the Convention for Women's Rights, held in Seneca Falls in July of that year, the resolutions adopted consistently reflected the Pragmatic position. The women and men assembled resolved "That woman is man's equal—was intended to be so by the Creator and the highest good of the race demands that she should be recognized as such."[6] They further passed a Declaration of Sentiments that enumerated the ways in which men had inflicted repeated injuries on women to establish an "absolute tyranny" over them. A central complaint was the denial by men of women's "inalienable right to the elective franchise."[7] Other wrongs that deserved redress included forcing women to submit to laws women had no part in making, denying civil rights to both married and single women, denying all property rights to women, prohibiting women from receiving an education or from pursuing high-paying and high-status occupations, establishing different moral standards for men and women, and destroying women's self-confidence and self-respect. In light of these injustices, the women at Seneca Falls declared themselves resolved to use political action to educate women about the laws under which they live, to encourage women to take an active role in public affairs, and to secure the vote for women.[8]

A basic belief of the Pragmatic Feminists is that if injustices are articulated, brought from the unstated realm of traditional behavior and subjected to rational debate, women will be able to mobilize and, as a majority, obtain their civil, political, and economic rights. More recently, the Pragmatic Feminist view has provided much of the motivating force behind the leadership of the National Organization for Women and the Equal Rights Amendment drive. The entire enterprise of the Pragmatic Feminists is to take women and issues that affect women out of what traditionally in the Constitution has been treated as the private sphere and to make these sex-gender issues a public matter. While Pragmatic Feminists are not revolutionary in the sense of expecting drastic social change to result from their actions, they do expect that numerous small changes which put women on a more equal footing with men will lead to major social changes. Just as many in the suffrage movement did not believe that the franchise would dramatically alter the status of women, many of the Pragmatic Feminists do not believe that passage of the Equal Rights Amendment would have destroyed the sex-gender organization of society. They do believe that the Nineteenth Amendment to the Constitution was a pragmatic step in the right direction that has made and will continue to make possible additional steps toward equality for women. In the tradition of American politics, Pragmatic Feminists deemphasize ideological positions with regard to other issues such as sexuality or socializing the economy; they even avoid spelling out the changes in interpersonal relations which the granting of their own demands will entail. The aim is to set specific practical goals that have a reasonable chance of winning majority agreement according to the accepted procedures of the existing political and economic system. The idea is not to change the system but rather to make it operate as it should.

Strategies for the Pragmatic Feminists

The work for ratification of the Equal Rights Amendment epitomizes the strategy of the Pragmatic Feminists who above all want equal treatment and equal opportunity for women. They believe that the best way to achieve this goal is to work pragmatically within the existing political system. Tactics involve organizing women, lobbying for legislation that will open economic, political, and educational opportunities for women, pushing for the appointment of women to high-status jobs in business and government, and developing networks of women who can help one another. Pragmatic Feminists are united in their belief that women are oppressed and that they must unite to work within the system for concrete changes. The National Organization for Women, founded in 1966, was the first of these groups. The National Women's Political Caucus, founded in 1971, is a similar organization composed of very politically sophisticated women who have been active as government officials, elected political leaders, labor-union leaders, and political-party activists. The organization raises money for candidates, lobbies to get women appointed to political and judicial positions, identifies women's issues, and lobbies to bring about favorable legislation for women.[9] In 1979, Pragmatic Feminists in New York, namely Gloria Steinem and Bella Abzug, made an effort to establish a women's network called Women, USA for the purpose of raising money among wealthy and professionally successful women and men to finance a women's newsletter and a toll-free telephone number for busy women to call to learn about the most current women's issues that need support and lobbying attention. Women, USA plans to focus on women's economic issues while pushing to get women into higher political and economic positions.[10]

The emergence of the New Right in the 1980 elections and the increased activity of the Right to Life movement in introducing a variety of anti-abortion laws in various state legislatures pushed NOW into a defensive stance. The defense of women's right to control their own bodies has become a central issue in the 1980s, overshadowing to some extent the economic issues.

Antifeminist Arguments

Antifeminist arguments hold that the inferior position of women in society derives from intrinsic biological differences between males and females. From these basic biological or anatomical differences derive psychological, economic, legal, and social differences. The explanations for the biological differences vary. Some ascribe them to a decree of God or some other religious entity. Others deem the differences simply a fact of nature. Antifeminists believe that the fundamental differences between the sexes are immutable, as also are the social and psychological patterns that have developed because of these differences. Antifeminists tend to articulate and define the role of women in response to feminist challenges that question and criticize previously uncontroversial social and political practices.

When women who had identity under the law only through their male relatives or husbands, who had practically no access to higher education, who often had no opportunity even to learn to read, and who were confined to work only as mothers, housekeepers, or unskilled or semiskilled laborers, began to question their status in society, antifeminists generally responded by citing religion or nature as the authority that opposed such changes.

When feminists demanded education, antifeminists declared women intellectually inferior, genetically and psychologically unable to be rational.

If feminists demanded political rights, the antifeminists declared women primarily fit for childbearing and child care, roles defined as incompatible with political activities.

When feminists demanded economic independence, antifeminists declared women physically frail, genetically passive in temperament, intellectually inferior, and psychologically unstable, qualities that make women suited only for the most menial and mindless economic tasks.

When feminists demanded readily available birth-control devices or safe abortions, antifeminists declared such technical and medical aid contrary to God's will.[11]

While religious arguments to counter feminist demands are numerous and seem to vary among Protestant sects according to the extent to which the image of the human body is incorporated into the ritual and belief of the sect,[12] scientific arguments based on nature undergird some of the most widely accepted antifeminist positions. Sigmund Freud's work, for example, is often cited as a "scientific" view which holds that men and women's psychic differences result from the anatomical differences between men and women and the way in which boys and girls respond to those differences. Freud's girls feel envy of the male penis. Freud's boys, on seeing a female, feel fear at the possibility of castration. Freud outlines the different responses girls and boys make to this biologically given situation. These reactions help shape in complicated ways the distinct psyches of males and females.[13]

Still another scientific biological view of women's inferiority is sociobiology, which finds genetic reasons for behavioral phenomena. Most antifeminists who use these theories and explanations consider them an absolute and ahistorical scientific description of the male and female psyches, and not an historically specific patriarchal order. Antifeminists, in general, always maintain that the differences between the sexes are fundamental and unchanging.

The Radical Feminist Perspective

The Radical Feminist position which emerged in the late 1960s holds that women are not only imprisoned by the laws of the society, but also and more significantly that they are entrapped and more deeply oppressed by the traditional organization of society according to sex and gender. Radical Feminists call the male-dominated organization of society the "patriarchy." Changing the law will only scratch the surface of the male-dominated social organization. While Radical Feminists differ among themselves in identifying the origins of the sex-gender system, all agree that the origins are extremely deep-rooted. Surprisingly, some Radical Feminists agree somewhat with the antifeminists on the biological origins of what Radical Feminists call the "patriarchy." The Pragmatic solution simply is not adequate because its basic assumption that equal political rights for women will give women political equality is wrong. For many like Shulamith Firestone, the origin of women's oppression is in the reproductive process. Women have traditionally had to cope with pregnancy, childbirth, menstruation, breast feeding, and infant care, all of which are physically draining enterprises. Prior to the advent of birth-control techniques, biological considerations completely dominated the lives of women, creating a division of labor that made women a separate caste as well as a separate economic class, dependent for survival upon men. The basic reproductive differences between men and women have structured economic, ideological, and psychological differences between men and women.[14] Radical Feminists resurrected Simone de Beauvoir's *The Second Sex*, written in 1949, to find an existential, psychological, and biological origin for women's inferiority.[15] For de Beauvoir, men originally defined women as an "other" primarily because women were tied to nature in their reproductive capacities. Whereas men were free to choose and to define themselves through their own actions, women were not able to be free in this existential sense. Related to this biological reproductive difference between men and women is the notion that men are genetically more aggressive than women and that this difference accounts for the basic social differences that pertain to the sexes.

While Pragmatic Feminists have found the identification of such fundamental biological and genetic differences to be counterproductive because of their seeming immutability, some Radical Feminists insist that technology can change these biological and genetic differences. Birth-control techniques and safe abortions have already made an impact. Children will eventually be conceived and nurtured outside of the womb. All child-oriented tasks will then devolve equally on males and females as society is revolutionized.[16] Meanwhile, the task for Radical Feminists involves breaking out of traditional cultural sex-gender relationships at every level of social interaction—sexual relations, family relations, relations with other women, work relations—and also out of presumably apolitical cultural expressions such as art, music, theater, film, history, language, and literature. Radical Feminists reject the notion of a public and a private sphere. Their message is that the private *is* the public, that politics is personal and is reflected in all aspects of the society, in language and through personal relations as well as in more traditionally recognized political and economic relations.

Strategies for Radical Feminists

In pursuing sexual freedom, many Radical Feminists can find a few precursors in such nineteenth-century feminists as Victoria Woodhull, a journalist, financier, and politician who worked for women's suffrage and for women's labor rights and who was an early advocate of free love. However, most nineteenth-century feminists were still heavily immersed in Victorian attitudes toward sexuality which advocated chastity if not celibacy for all. Many of the Radical Feminists of the 1960s have pioneered in this area by advocating separatism for women in the form of lesbianism.[17] These women view lesbianism as a political and psychological necessity. Women must seek new ways of sexual expression free of male domination. Lesbians who are a part of the Radical Feminist faction argue that they severely challenge male dominance because they have no need for males. Their very existence breaks the subordinate-superordinate relationship of the established sex-gender system. Lesbianism can politically unite women, because competition among women for men is the most divisive aspect of patriarchal society that prevents heterosexual women from being politically unified. For other Radical Feminists, challenging modes of sexuality may mean trying to develop heterosexual interactions that deemphasize the genitals, deemphasize sexual performance and the specific act of intercourse, in favor of a broader involvement of all the senses. In this regard, not only women but men also must change their notions of sexuality.

Marriage, the family, and romantic ideas of love and motherhood are other institutions that Radical Feminists attack. In addition to bearing and nursing children, women have had the principal responsibility for childrearing and socialization practices. Radical Feminists argue that marriage as an institution is a model for all other forms of discrimination against women. Until very recently, a married woman has had no civil rights, has had no sexual rights, and has been forced to be a "slave" to her husband in performing all cleaning, cooking, washing, food purchasing, and child-care chores without being paid for her services.

Some Radical Feminists find the psychic relationship which develops between mother and child to be a repressive and oppressive influence that dominates society and culture and structures all social relations in ways that are repressive. Dorothy Dinerstein argues that the domination of early childhood by females structures the pattern of complementarity between male and female personalities in the patriarchal order.[18] The power of women in this situation is a kind of negative power. Women have the impressive biological power of childbearing. Because this power depends upon the sexual vigor of males, women foster male self-respect and allow males to have the main responsibility for history.[19] This motive explains the willingness of women to extoll and accept ideological myths such as romantic love, femininity, and motherhood. Dinerstein, like many Radical Feminists, believes that the sex-gender organization of society supports a host of other kinds of oppression, including racism, imperialism, and the scientific "machine" culture of Western civilization that worships the mechanical and denigrates the organic and the living. Firestone makes similar claims to support the thesis that the reorganization of the gender system in society will revolutionize the economic, the technical, and the cultural aspects of society as well as the nature of personal interrelationships.

On the question of work, many Radical Feminists accept what resembles a Marxian analysis of the economy; however, they assign economics to a separate if not dependent role in relation to the sex-gender system. Radical Feminists see capitalism as a patriarchal development and not *vice-versa*. This basic difference, of course, makes Radical Feminists quite at odds with Marxists. Culture is perhaps more important to the

Radical Feminists than work or economic concerns. Language, art, music, and history, the ideology of the society as it is played out in people's unconscious, is more fundamental than even the economy. The operation of the economy, in fact, depends upon accepted unarticulated assumptions about gender. The way to unravel this interdependence is not to attack the economic organization of the society but rather to attack the content of the collective unconscious as it manifests itself in cultural affairs. Women, because they are outside the system, have a special knowledge of reality that can offer significant insights into the new directions which society must take. Women's art, music, literature, and other forms of self-expression must be supported and encouraged. Women in business and in the professions must do their jobs in creative new ways that are not repressive and dominating but that break patriarchal relationships by convincing others that a feminist way is not only different and possible but also better.

The Socialist Feminist Position

The difference between the Radical Feminist position and the Socialist Feminist position is one of emphasis in that there is probably as much variation within each position as there is between the two categories.[20] Socialist Feminists agree with many of the assumptions of the Radical Feminists. They agree that the Pragmatic Feminist position does not take sufficient account of the deep-rooted nature of the sex-gender system in the society, that preserving the public and the private spheres of life to obtain legal equality and equal opportunities in the job market will not prevent the patriarchal system from operating in the private sphere and thereby maintaining its hegemony in the public sphere.

Both the Radical Feminists and the Socialist Feminists also agree that the traditional Marxist position with regard to women is wrong. The Marxist view holds that the oppression of women originates in the mode of production and in the social institution of private property. Engels's *The Origin of the Family, Private Property, and the State* provides the primary text for the Marxist position. Engels's identification of the patriarchal system with private property and the emergence of the nuclear family as an institution for securing property is rejected by both Radical and Socialist Feminists because it suggests that with a change in the capitalist mode of production the patriarchy will disappear. Furthermore, Engels argues that property is the only cause of women's oppression. Since the proletariat has no property, the proletariat has no concept of the family.[21]

4. The Minority Politics of Women

It is on the relationship of the sex-gender system to the economic mode of production that the Radical Feminist and the Socialist Feminist disagree. Radical Feminists hold that while capitalism is oppressive, the sex-gender system is even more oppressive. The sex-gender system has historical roots that antedate capitalism and are more ingrained in every aspect of the culture than is the economic mode of production. Socialist Feminists, in contrast, believe that there is a close interrelationship and interdependence in the various forms which the sex-gender system and the economic class system take at any given period in history. The two systems are not separate but are dialectically related to one another. At least some Radical Feminists ascribe to biological differences the origins of the sex-gender system, which is and has always been a patriarchy. Socialist Feminists look to social and symbolic organization as the cause of women's oppression and seek to extend the historical materialist method to analyze the relations of women as producers and reproducers and also to analyze the ideological formulations of these relations. The patriarchy is but one historically specific sex-gender system, just as capitalism is one historically specific organization of production.

Those interested in material relations tend to emphasize the work women do as wage laborers and as domestic laborers and to analyze the contradictions which these two forms of labor create. Marx did not discuss domestic labor. Domestic labor includes reproduction, childbearing, home maintenance, nurturing, and consumption. Socialist Feminists identify women as the moving force in breaking down the patriarchal organization of society just as the proletariat must be the agent that challenges the capitalist mode of production. Of concern is how domestic labor is related to the production of surplus value. Socialist Feminists argue that domestic labor is as essential for the operation of capitalism as wage labor. This means that a revolt against women's role as chief domestic has the potential of putting the economic order into disarray. The problem, of course, is how to develop either feminist consciousness or class consciousness when many women by virtue of their close connection to the patriarchy see themselves as having little in common with one another.

Some Socialist Feminists are more like the Radical Feminists in emphasizing the ideological structure of the sex-gender system. However, most Socialist Feminists see the patriarchy as an historically specific situation that has developed in a dialectical relationship with material conditions of production. Socialist Feminists attempt to integrate the political, economic, and psychological in their analyses and in their strategies. Some emphasize one system more than the other. Whereas the Marxist model can be altered to describe the economic conditions of women in a logical, conscious, and rational way, it does not help illuminate or explain the structure and operation of the sex-gender system, which is rooted in unarticulated aspects of the unconscious, in language, in culture and in symbol exchanges among people.

In this area some of the most interesting theoretical work is being done in the feminist movement. Using insights from the French structuralists and poststructuralists, Juliet Mitchell and Gayle Rubin have begun to explore how the symbolic ideological system is organized with regard to gender and how the system operates.[22] Drawing on the anthropological work of Lévi-Strauss, especially in his *The Elementary Structures of Kinship*, Gayle Rubin focuses attention on Lévi-Strauss's idea that the exchange of women is a fundamental principle of kinship that organizes relations of sex and gender. While objecting to Lévi-Strauss's claim that general rules that govern the exchange of women (such as the incest taboo, required heterosexuality, and the asymmetrical division of the sexes) constitute the origin of culture, Rubin does believe that these rules and the kinship systems which develop from them establish systems of social relationships which include certain rights and obligations for men and different rights and obligations for women. These sex-gender systems differ and have a "political economy" or life of their own, which needs analysis.

Lévi-Strauss's contribution is that he has identified gender systems as somewhat autonomous and has developed some concepts with which to analyze these gender systems in different situations. To understand how children come to know the conventions of the sex-gender system, it is necessary to study the way in which symbols are organized, the way in which the sexes are asymmetrical, and the way in which children are socialized into male and female roles in society.

Psychoanalysis provides some of the major concepts available in this enterprise. Psychoanalysis, according to Jacques Lacan, is the study of the traces left on the psyche by the socialization or enculturalization of the individual into kinship systems.[23] Both Rubin and Juliet Mitchell agree and both note that feminists have in the past misunderstood the meaning of Freud's terminology. Freud's theory is not an explanation of women's inferiority, but rather is is a theory explaining how the sex-gender system is organized and assimilated by both men and women in society and how the content of this system oppresses and subjugates women. Freud's oedipal concept is a description of how this dominance operates. The symbolic organization of the unconscious reflects, supports, and exists in a dialectical relationship with the material and social organization of the society.[24]

4. The Minority Politics of Women

Neither Rubin nor Mitchell accept Lévi-Strauss's structuralist proposition that sex-gender systems are ahistorical emanations of the human mind. Instead, they argue that sex-gender systems exist and operate interdependently with economic and political systems in historical relationships. The agenda is to engage in analyses that do not deal with one factor only, but rather attempt to take into account a multiplicity of interacting factors.

Of particular concern for Socialist Feminists is the organization of the sex-gender system as it is expressed in kinship systems. Mitchell argues that the patriarchal system did not originate because of women's reproductive roles. Neither is it the capitalist economy that demands a patriarchal sex-gender system. Rather it is the cultural use of women as exchange objects that assigns women to a feminine definition and gives fathers, not men, a determinant role.[25] Mitchell argues that capitalism makes kinship structure and incest taboos irrelevant and yet capitalism insists on preserving such structures of patriarchy. The realm of the patriarchy is the unconscious that Freud analyzed. It exists in each individual. The unconscious is also the domain in which culture, ideology, and symbols are reproduced. The nuclear family is at the heart of the contradiction that exists between the oedipal complex and the incest and other taboos of the nuclear family. This is the fundamental contradiction that women must analyze and use to overthrow the patriarchy.

Women have to organize themselves as a group to effect a change in the basic ideology of human society. To be effective, this can be no righteous challenge to the simple domination of men (though this plays a tactical part), but a struggle based on a theory of the social non-necessity at this stage of development of the laws instituted by the patriarchy.[26]

The nuclear family is the institution that continues to mitigate the contradiction which exists between patriarchal rules and the social organization of work.[27] While the patriarchy, like capitalism, is "in the slow death throes of its own irrationality," only a political struggle can bring down either capitalism or the patriarchy. Since the patriarchy is not the same as capitalism, the gains or losses in the two systems will be interdependent and uneven. The patriarchy and capitalism exist in something of a dialectical relationship. This explains why socialist countries like Russia and China have not yet eliminated the patriarchy. These countries have not completed their socialist revolutions as the laws and culture of patriarchy still persist. Women must insist on a new organization of the unconscious.[28]

Others of Socialist Feminist persuasion emphasize the contradictions that exist between the patriarchal rules and the social organization of work. In an earlier book, Juliet Mitchell discusses the work women do in capitalist society as involving four basic functions: production, reproduction, sexuality, and the socialization of children. [29] The reproductive capacity of women has resulted in a situation in which the unpaid labor of women is necessary to the operation of capitalism. In other words, capitalism needs patriarchy. For any significant change to occur, the structure of all four functions must change. To change only the production function for women might in fact increase repression in one or all of the other structures. For a true transformation to occur, all four structures must rupture. The task of the Socialist Feminist is to analyze the uneven development of each structure and attack the weakest link in the combination.[30]

Building on Mitchell's line of argument, Zillah R. Eisenstein has added the functions of home maintenance and consumption as areas of activity and struggle for women. She argues that the strategy for Socialist Feminists cannot follow classical Marxist lines but rather that women must organize political consciousness and action around the ways in which their oppression grows out of daily struggles. These include trying to work in the labor force for lesser wages, reproducing children who become new workers, providing nurturing for children as well as for men in society, and providing markets for the products of capitalism as consumers. The idea is that if women can invent a mode of analysis to explain and comprehend their own daily lives, such an analysis will be able to transform women's lives.[31]

Putting the same idea in a slightly different way, Ann Foreman argues that the liberal separation of the public from the private, the political from the personal, is an ideological belief that traditional Marxism did not challenge and that is responsible for the oppression of women.[32] By refusing to separate the public from the private, by recognizing that the personal is political, the women's movement makes an enormous contribution in transforming the location, the content, and the form of political struggle. Women can extend the struggle beyond the trade unions into all organizations of the society; they can use women's issues such as abortion and child care to raise questions about the inevitability of fundamental concepts such as genital sexuality and heterosexuality. In other words, women's issues are extremely important not only in and of themselves, but they are important because they raise more fundamental questions about the sex-gender organization of society, questions that must be addressed. Finally, Foreman argues that by organizing into autonomous units within political structures, women can mobilize women to prevent their oppression and exclusion.[33]

Strategies for Socialist Feminists

Drawing on these theoretical ideas, Socialist Feminists work politically in a variety of arenas, most of which focus on patterns of interaction, habits, speech, images, symbols, and laws that affect the everyday lives of women. Socialist Feminists identify very readily with the needs of workers in the labor force, especially female workers. They agitate and organize to encourage women to become conscious of their economic oppression as women and as workers. To help women gain control over their reproductive lives, many Socialist Feminists have joined with Radical Feminists in pressing for the legalization of abortion. Campaigning to expose the symbolic and ideological trappings of the patriarchy is another priority for Socialist Feminists. The treatment of women as sex objects, the association of sexuality with violence, the perpetuation of images that associate both men and women with explicit sex-determined roles in the economy and in the patriarchy are all targets that must be demystified and eliminated from the arts, from literature, from school books, from advertising, and from the media in general. In addition, child-care centers, battered-women centers, rape workshops, hotlines, assertiveness training, and consciousness raising are all part of the agenda for Socialist Feminists.

A large portion of the Socialist Feminists regarded the Equal Rights Amendment as being insignificant or even detrimental to the cause of women. Socialist Feminists argued that the major focus of the women's movement must take place in the personal and what has been traditionally considered the "private" spheres of life. Just as the voting-rights amendment did not change the condition of women in the United States (and also, once passed, eliminated the major organizing focus for women), many Socialist Feminists believed the passage of the Equal Rights Amendment would have the same effect. It would become a symbolic token that would defuse the women's movement. Other Socialist Feminists supported the Equal Rights Amendment not as a panacea or solution but as a small contributing factor in the ideological and psychic struggle that is necessary for a meaningful cultural and economic revolution.

With some exceptions, the differences between Pragmatic, Radical, and Socialist Feminists lie not so much in the political activities each group pursues as in the definition of what the women's movement can achieve and in the evaluation of what constitutes a "success" or a "failure." Pragmatic Feminists look to the political, legal, and economic areas. They want to see women in responsible jobs with equal pay for equal work, with equal political rights, and equal opportunities for participation. Psychic identity and oppression are certainly recognized as important problems, but not the main or only problems. Radical Feminists stress that the private is public, that the psychic identity of men and women as organized in the sex-gender system has an integrity of its own that is more pervasive and deep rooted in the human psyche than are the economic and political arrangements of the society. It is the sex-gender system, the patriarchy, the psychic identities of men and women, that must be attacked. Finally, the Socialist Feminists see the women's movement as a kind of replacement or supplement to the proletariat in the political ideological struggle of oppressed peoples against their oppressors. Ultimately, it will result in a new form of social and political organization as well as in a new and different form of psychic organization. Particular political activities or strategies must be evaluated in a much broader historical context, according to the Socialist Feminists. A material gain for women may entail a psychic or symbolic loss. Socialist Feminists believe that they must establish and evaluate political strategies, recognizing that both material and psychic universes are involved and that while the two realms are interdependent, elimination of the patriarchy requires a constant vigilance with regard to the domain of the unconscious, the personal, the symbolic, and the psyche.

Notes for Chapter 4

1. For a more comprehensive treatment of women in American history see Eleanor Flexner, *Century of Struggle* (New York: Atheneum, 1971). For a less voluminous account see Barbara Sinclair Deckard, *The Women's Movement: Political, Socioeconomic, and Psychological Issues* (New York: Harper, 1979).

2. Deckard, p. 319. See also *Handbook on Women Workers*, Women's Bureau, U.S. Department of Labor (Washington, D.C.: U.S. Government Printing Office, 1969). p. 10.

3. Deckard, pp. 343–345.

4. Deckard, pp. 346–349.

5. Deckard, pp. 350–352.

6. "Proceedings of the Woman's Rights Conventions, Rochester, New York,

August 2, 1848," in *Woman's Rights Conventions, Seneca Falls and Rochester, 1848* (New York: Arno and the *New York Times*, 1969), p. 5.

7. "Proceedings of the Woman's Rights Conventions," p. 5.

8. "Proceedings of the Woman's Rights Conventions," p. 5.

9. Deckard, p. 366 (note 1 above).

10. Joy Horowitz, "Coast to Coast Woman's Network," *Los Angeles Times* 3 July 1979, Sec. 5, p. 1.

11. See *Feminist Frameworks: Alternative Theoretical Accounts of the Relations between Women and Men*, eds. Alison M. Jagger and Paula A. Rothenberg Struhl (New York: McGraw-Hill, 1978), pp. 86-98; 174-177; 226-235; 278-284.

12. Howard Happ, "American Denominations: Civilized and Primitive," unpublished paper delivered at Institute for Teaching and Learning Seminar, California State University, Northridge, 19 March 1979.

13. For an example of an essay which when read literally would support the antifeminist position, see Sigmund Freud, "Femininity," *New Introductory Lectures on Psychoanalysis*, ed. James Strachey (New York: Norton, 1933), pp. 158-184.

14. Shulamith Firestone, *The Dialectic of Sex: The Case for Feminist Revolution* (New York: Bantam, 1970).

15. Simone de Beauvoir, *The Second Sex*, trans. H. M. Parshley (New York: Bantam Books, 1968).

16. Firestone (note 14 above).

17. Charlotte Bunch, "Lesbians in Revolt," reprinted in Jagger and Struhl, pp. 135-142 (note 11 above).

18. Dorothy Dinerstein, *The Mermaid and the Minotaur: Sexual Arrangements and Human Malaise* (New York: Harper, 1976).

19. Dinerstein, pp. 212-213.

20. For a good discussion of the difference between Radical Feminism and Socialist Feminism, see Jagger and Struhl, pp. 83-85 (note 11 above). Representatives of the Socialist Feminist position include Zillah R. Eisenstein, ed., *Capitalist Patriarchy and the Case for Socialist Feminism* (New York: Monthly Review Press, 1979) and Ann Foreman, *Femininity as Alienation: Women and the Family in Marxism and Psychoanalysis* (London, Pluto Press, 1977).

21. Friedrich Engels, *The Origin of the Family, Private Property, and the State.* For a discussion of the Socialist Feminist critique of Engels, see Foreman, pp. 25-29.

22. Gayle Rubin, "The Traffic in Women: Notes on the Political Economy of

Sex," in *Toward an Anthropology of Women*, ed. Rayna R. Reiter (New York: Monthly Review Press, 1975), pp. 157–210. Juliet Mitchell, *Psychoanalysis and Feminism: Freud, Reich, Laing, and Women* (New York: Vintage, 1975).

23. Jacques Lacan, *The Language of the Self: The Function of Language in Psychoanalysis*, trans. Anthony Wilden (Baltimore: Johns Hopkins University Press, 1968).

24. Mitchell, p. xiii; also Rubin, pp. 158–159 (note 22 above).

25. Mitchell, pp. 407–409.

26. Mitchell, p. 414.

27. Mitchell, p. 413.

28. Mitchell, p. 415.

29. Juliet Mitchell, *Woman's Estate* (New York: Pantheon Books, 1971), especially pp. 99–122.

30. Mitchell, *Woman's Estate*, p. 122.

31. Zillah R. Eisenstein, "Developing a Theory of Capitalist Patriarchy," in Eisenstein, pp. 5–40 (note 20 above).

32. Foreman, p. 154 (note 20 above).

33. Foreman, pp. 154–158.

Chapter 5

The Minority Politics of the Chicanos

Geography, economics, and history are key factors that define the strategic position of Chicanos in United States politics. Mexico is a bordering nation whose economy is much less developed than that of the United States. United States multinational businesses have established numerous ties with Mexico that exploit Mexican labor and natural resources. These international political and economic relationships between Mexico and the United States set the parameters for Chicano minority politics within the United States. As with Jewish or Japanese minorities at different times in United States history, the strategic situation of Chicanos varies with international economic interdependencies. Today, Chicanos as an interest group increasingly translate the situation of Mexico and other Third World countries into substantive domestic issues in the United States.

Of critical importance to the strategic position of Chicanos is the history of Chicano settlement in what is now the United States.[1] Mexican explorers were among the first foreign settlers in what has become United States territory. These explorers found ways of surviving the winters of the barren Southwest by moving in on the Pueblo Indian settlements in what is now New Mexico. Santa Fe, founded in 1609, is one of the oldest cities in the United States. Mestizos (mixed Spanish and Indian blood) also settled in California, in Texas, and in Arizona. Each of these communities developed in relative isolation. Indian raiders cut off east-west communications between the settlements in North America, forcing communication and travel to follow a fan-like pattern from Mexico to the North. The economic and geographic circumstances of each area consequently tended to influence the social and political development of each region somewhat separately in a way that continues to characterize Chicano politics today. Political tactics that work in Texas, for example, may not work well in California or New Mexico because the economics, history, and social organization of each area differs from the others.

Today, Mexican Americans live in every state in the Union; however, about 80 percent of them are concentrated in the southwestern states of Texas, New Mexico, Colorado, Arizona, and California. Obtaining accurate demographic figures for Mexican Americans is extremely difficult, as the census records distinguish only according to Spanish surname. This practice lumps together all those of Latin American descent, including Puerto Ricans, Cubans, and other Caribbean peoples. The 1980 Census figures show the Spanish-surname population to number around 14 million. However, these figures do not include undocumented immigrants, recent arrivals, children, and many who were not counted by the Census. Some estimates suggest the number of Spanish-surname individuals to be around 15 million. Of these, possibly 11 million are of Mexican heritage; these constitute about 5 percent of the total United States population. In the five southwestern states, however, Chicanos constitute around 19 percent of the population. In the Southwestern, Mountain, and Western states, Spanish-surname individuals outnumber Blacks and are the largest minority ethnic group in the region (See Table 1). The influx of immigrants from south of the

Table 1
Distribution of Spanish-Surname and Black Populations
in Five Southwestern States
(in thousands)

	Total	Race White	Race Black	Race Other	Spanish surname* Number	Spanish surname* Percent
California	23,669	18,032	1,819	3,818	4,544	19
Texas	14,228	11,198	1,710	1,320	2,986	21
New Mexico	1,300	976	24	299	476	37
Arizona	2,718	2,240	75	403	441	16
Colorado	2,889	2,571	102	217	339	12
U.S.	226,505	188,341	26,488	11,676	14,606	6

Figures taken from U.S. Census, Twentieth, 1980 Population, Supplementary Reports, PC80-S1-1, *Age, Sex, Race, and Spanish Origin of the Population by Regions, Divisions, and States: 1980* (Washington, D.C.: U.S. Government Printing Office, 1981), p. 6.

*Persons of Spanish surname may be of any race, i.e. White, Black or Other.

border, combined with the high birth rates for Spanish-speaking populations in the United States, have caused demographers to estimate that Hispanics will surpass Blacks as the largest minority ethnic group in the United States in the mid-1980s.[2] While information is extremely limited, probably well over three-fourths of these individuals will be of Mexican descent. The long-established historical experience of Mexican Americans in the Southwest, combined with the increasingly rapid growth of the Spanish-speaking population in the United States and the changing economic relationships between the United States and Mexico, make the strategic position of the Chicanos a particularly complex and dynamic political phenomenon.

A Brief History

While the social and political organization of the early Mexican communities in the seventeenth and eighteenth centuries were quite different from one another in New Mexico, California, Texas, and Arizona, they were all hierarchical in nature and exhibited many vestiges of feudal organization.[3] This was particularly true of New Mexico, where a relatively stable agrarian society operated with a barter economy and a fairly rigid class structure composed of landed gentry *(ricos)*, a small class of farmers, herders, traders, and merchants, and a larger class of peasants.[4] In Texas, where ranching provided a somewhat nomadic life style, the class structure was not so apparent. Large landowners dealt with one another on a fairly equal basis, while the number of ranch hands, traders, and merchants was limited.[5] In California, a fairly hierarchical society developed where light-skinned Mestizos of Spanish heritage composed the patron class and many of the native Indians were enslaved.[6] Between these two extremes were cowboys, artisans, farmers, and merchants. The small Mexicano settlement in Arizona was continually under attack by the Apache Indians and never established a long-term community.[7]

The conquest of the Southwest by Anglo Americans began in the early nineteenth century with the opening of the Santa Fe Trail in 1820 and the simultaneous expansion of the western frontier into Texas. In 1830, the Mexican government became alarmed at the influx of Anglos and issued a decree which prohibited the further colonization of Texas by Anglos. The Anglo Americans already settled in the territory responded in 1836 by declaring themselves an independent republic. Mexico sent troops into Texas, which were met by the Texas pioneers under Sam Houston. South Texas became a battleground.[8] In 1846, the United States declared war on Mexico, defeated the Mexican army, and in 1848, Mexico and the United States signed the Treaty of Guadalupe Hidalgo. This treaty ceded to the United States most of what is now Texas, California, Nevada, New Mexico, Utah, and parts of Colorado and Wyoming. In spite of the guarantees in the Treaty of Guadalupe Hidalgo, the influx of Anglos combined with the history of violence and hatred in South Texas pushed the Mexicanos into a minority status. In New Mexico, Anglos used Anglo law and a money-based taxation system to disrupt the barter economy of the Mexicanos and force them off their land into the migrant labor force. The expanding railroad system absorbed much of this labor.[9] In California, the gold rush of 1849 brought an influx of Anglos who overwhelmed and eventually destroyed the existing Mexicano communities. By the end of 1849, over 80,000 Anglos had come to California to join the approximately 7500 Mexicanos already living there. In Northern California, the Mexicanos were immediately reduced to a minority; in Southern California, the Spanish-speaking Californios were able to maintain their control only for another twenty years.[10]

Between 1870 and 1900, the frontier expanded, railroads were completed, and the United States Army defeated the Apache, Navaho, and Comanche Indians. All of these developments enabled agricultural production to increase dramatically in the Southwest. Farmland tripled in acreage while land under irrigation doubled. Cotton production moved across Texas into New Mexico and California, creating a demand for more agricultural labor. Sugar-beet production in Colorado and in the Midwest also expanded. Mexicans (many of them undocumented) and Mexican Americans provided much of the labor for these crops in addition to providing much of the labor that built the railroads in the Southwest.[11]

While the flow of Mexican migration into the United States prior to 1900 numbered in the hundreds, in the twentieth century several million Mexicans have crossed the border, especially between the periods of 1900 to 1930, and 1942 to the present.[12] As Carey McWilliams has noted, the pattern of employment for Mexican labor in the Southwest has been primarily provided by large-scale industrial enterprises such as the railroads, sugar-beet refineries, and large fruit and vegetable cultivation. The employers hired Mexican labor in groups—as gangs, crews, or families—to perform the most undesirable unskilled work. Mexican labor performed jobs in undesirable locations (such as laying railroad ties in the desert) and filled seasonal positions. Employers provided separate camps and somewhat segregated job opportunities.[13] Conditions of poverty and debt peonage in Mexico combined with the availability of jobs in the United States. The jobs were in mines, on railroads, and in beet, citrus, cotton, and vegetable fields.[14]

With the depression of the 1930s, migration stopped. Instead, the United States government deported over 350,000 persons of Mexican descent (including United States citizens) to Mexico between 1931 and 1934 in an effort to reduce competition among the unemployed for scarce jobs.[15] Not until the United States entered World War II did the United States again welcome Mexicans, primarily to work in agricultural jobs created by the wartime economy. The United States fostered this migration with its bracero program (Public Law 45), which went into effect in 1942 and lasted until 1964.[16] The purpose of the program was to bring Mexican nationals as contract labor into the United States to work for short periods of time varying from 45 days to 6 months. Men came without their families and were supposed to return to Mexico when their contracts expired. In 1943, approximately 53,000 persons were involved in the bracero program. The expanding need for labor in the United States caused the number contracted on the program to increase to around 400,000 a year from 1955 to 1964.[17] In addition, a considerable number of "illegal" migrants or "wetbacks," who were not a part of the bracero program, also crossed the border. Many who came as braceros managed to return to the United States illegally. Although figures are obviously not available, some estimate of the dimensions of the problem comes from the fact that between 1942 and 1954, 1,329,741 braceros were contracted while 3,371,374 undocumented aliens were deported.[18] During the period 1942 to 1964, over 4.5 million Mexican nationals, including many repeaters, came to the United States on the program.[19] The bracero program continued the pattern of group employment established in the earlier part of the century. The end of the bracero program in 1964 did not stop the flow of people north across the border.

Problems in Counting Undocumented Immigrants

Trying to establish even the approximate number of undocumented workers who have come to the United States in recent years is a guessing game involving large variations. Estimates range from 2 to 12 million persons, of which 60 percent are Mexican. The remainder come from other Latin American countries.[20] A figure of 5.2 million provided by Lesko Associates, a private firm under contract to the Immigration and Naturalization Service in 1975, has been attacked by many experts as being too high.[21] Still another factor involves how many of these undocumented workers stay as permanent residents in the United States and how many return to Mexico, their country of origin, usually after a short time. In spite of these uncertainties, most officials and experts agree that the new flow of undocumented people into the United States from

Mexico has been at least as many as 100,000 a year since 1964.[22] This fact is extremely important in establishing the strategic political position of Chicanos as an interest group in the United States. Undocumented workers come into the United States seeking jobs and a better standard of living. Many come to join relatives who are already settled in the United States. In summarizing the results of four independent studies of apprehended undocumented Mexican workers (with sample sizes ranging from 481 to 2794) done in 1969, 1972, 1975, and 1977, David North and Marion Houstoun describe undocumented workers as being young (around 27 to 28 years old), mostly male, poorly educated (less than 6 years of primary education), employed in low-paying, unskilled jobs, and mostly from rural areas in Mexico.[23]

Other studies note that since 1964, undocumented workers are much more likely to seek the higher wages and easier working conditions available in urban areas far from the border rather than attempt to obtain agricultural work.[24] While accurate information is not available, it is clear that new immigrants head for existing Chicano communities within the United States where they may have relatives or contacts.

Political Organization among Chicanos Today

While many Mexican Americans participated in the nascent labor movement in the United States during the early 1900s by striking against the gold and silver mines, the railroads, and the cotton, sugar beet, melon, and berry growers, the political organization of Mexican Americans as such had a late start. As was mentioned above, the fanlike settlement of Mexicans in Texas, New Mexico, California, and Colorado has influenced the structure of Chicano political organization today. Poverty combined with the threat of deportation made organizing very difficult in all areas.

Not surprisingly, the first Mexican American organization developed in Texas, where the economy supported a larger middle-class Mexican American population. The League of United Latin American Citizens (LULAC) was founded in Texas in 1927 as a middle-class organization devoted to promoting the interests and rights of Mexican Americans.[25] After World War II, also in Texas, Mexican American veterans formed the G.I. Forum to fight acts of discrimination against Mexican Americans in the Veterans Administration and in general. By 1949, the G.I. Forum had established over 100 Forums in Texas. In 1974, the organization had branches in 23 states and a membership of more than 20,000. Activities of the group include lobbying to place Mexican Americans in appointive

5. The Minority Politics of the Chicanos 91

and in elective offices. The group also supports community-service activities.[26]

At about the same time the G.I. Forum was organizing in Texas, Saul Alinsky founded the Community Services Organization (CSO) in 1947, to organize poor urban Mexican Americans in California. Cesar Chavez was a member of the Community Services Organization in his early days before he decided to try to organize migrant farmworkers.[27]

However, it was not until the 1960s, with the rising militancy of the Black civil-rights movement, that indigenous Chicano organizations began to emerge in larger numbers. The Mexican American Political Association (MAPA) developed in 1958 in California as a middle-class organization concerned with asserting the political muscle of the Mexican American population.[28] In 1963, Mexican Americans in Crystal City, Texas, founded the Political Association of Spanish Speaking Organizations (PASSO), whose aim was to win some local seats on the Crystal City School Board to represent Mexican Americans in a small town whose population was 80 to 90 percent Mexican American. This later developed into La Raza Unida Party in Texas, committed to winning local and state offices for Mexican American citizens. The Party has been successful in winning elections in numerous Chicano towns in South Texas and has organized in California also.[29] By 1965, Cesar Chavez had mobilized his National Farm Workers Association (later the United Farm Workers) to call for a strike in Delano, California. In New Mexico, a former preacher, Reies López Tijerina, organized La Alianza de Pueblos Libres which launched a campaign demanding compensation for the "land grab" which Anglos had perpetrated after the Treaty of Guadalupe Hidalgo.[30] In Colorado, Rodolfo "Corky" Gonzalez organized Chicano youth into La Cruzada para la Justicia.[31] Neighborhood centers developed in East Los Angeles, San Diego, Berkeley, San Antonio, El Paso, and Denver, along with mutual-aid societies, literary clubs, credit unions, art centers, local newspapers, and Spanish publications. In 1968, the Black movement and the Chicano movement began focusing on the universities. Chicano college students formed the United Mexican American Students (UMAS), Mexican American Youth Organization (MAYO), and Movimiento Estudiantil Chicano de Aztlán (MECHA) to recruit Chicano youth to the university.[32] The Mexican American Legal Defense Fund (MALDEF) was founded in 1968, in San Antonio, Texas, as a Mexican American counterpart to the National Association for the Advancement of Colored People. This has now become a national organization with offices in Los Angeles, San Francisco, San Antonio, and Washington, D.C.

During the 1970s, numerous other organizations representing Chicano interests emerged such as the Mexican American Women's National Association, the National Council of La Raza and the Hispanic Lawyers Association. In December, 1979, the Hispanic American Democrats (HAD) held a founding convention in Denver in an attempt to unite all Spanish-speaking peoples in the United States; Chicanos, Puerto Ricans, and Cuban Americans met for the purpose of building a political caucus within the Democratic Party.[33]

The Strategic Position of Chicanos

The strategic position of Chicanos in the United States is defined by the history of Mexican settlement in the United States, by the economic conditions that have made Mexican labor a vital part of the United States economy, and by the divided political consciousness and political identity of the Mexican American population. In spite of the pervasive Anglo stereotype of the Mexican—as lazy, uneducated, dirty, lawless, and uncultured, which dominated the public media, the schools, and the history books prior to 1970—many Mexican Americans have accepted the Lockean Liberal ideal whereby individuals status is conferred by individual productivity and individual effort. Mexican Americans of this sort have supported Richard Nixon, Gerald Ford, and Sam Yorty in various elections during the 1960s and early 1970s.

Another portion of the Mexican American population has traditionally rejected or been forced to reject the Anglo-assimilation role. Carey McWilliams, writing in 1948, records a split within the Mexican American community according to one's being a native-born United States citizen as opposed to an immigrant from Mexico. The native-born tend to consider themselves superior to the immigrants. United States natives called the immigrants "cholo" or "chicano," terms of derision, whereas the immigrants called the United States native-born a "pocho."[34] The group of individuals who refused to assimilate, sometimes known as the "pachucos" or "zoot suiters" in the 1930s and 1940s and gang members in the 1950s and 1960s, epitomize in their lifestyles a cultural rejection of the Lockean Liberal ethic. They serve as an "other" for Anglos and have been ridiculed, harassed, jailed, and sometimes deported.

A third portion of the Mexican American population is somewhat ambivalent about its relationship both to Anglo values and to identification with Mexico or with the Chicano movement.

The documented and undocumented workers who migrate from Mexico into the United States constitute a fourth component of the Mexican

5. The Minority Politics of the Chicanos

American population within the United States. These individuals are primarily Spanish speaking. Many of them leave their families in Mexico and return there at intervals. For them, Mexico is home, although some have eventually decided to settle in the United States.

This mix of political orientations makes the strategic situation of the Chicano movement very different from that of the Black movement in the United States. As a whole, Black people in the United States were and continue to be much more collectively aware of Anglo discrimination, racism, and the political strategies necessary for survival as a racial minority. Those who vote, vote as a bloc. Mexican Americans in the United States are historically a conquered but not an enslaved people. Economic conditions have attracted Mexicans to the United States. The movement back and forth across the border has helped to prevent a more complete collective identity of Mexican Americans as an oppressed minority within the United States. Indicative of this phenomenon is the split within the community concerning an appropriate name. The term "Mexican American" has long denoted an ethnic group that presumably would assimilate into American society much in the same way that Irish Americans or Polish Americans have assimilated. In New Mexico, the term "Hispanic American" has been preferred, with a general cultural reference to Spain. More recently, the terms "Hispanic" and "Latino" have been revived by the press to include Puerto Ricans and Cubans as well as Mexicans. During the 1960s a more militant element of the community, identifying themselves more with the pachucos and zoot suiters of the 1940s, chose to elevate as a source of pride the term "Chicano," which like "Black" had in the past been a term of derision. The Chicano movement of the 1960s and 1970s drew much of its inspiration from the Black and Afro-American movements.

One segment of this group has propagated a strong cultural nationalism by emphasizing the priority of the traditional Aztlán culture (the lost kingdom of the Aztecs) and advocating the reconquest of the southwestern United States by the Mexican race. This group views Mexican culture and the Spanish language as a basis for building a Chicano identity in the United States. Another segment of those who identify as Chicanos are in sympathy with a more straightforward Marxist explanation of their situation as a phenomenon generated by United States imperialism and the system of world capitalism.

Whereas most Americans of African heritage have developed a consensus that eschews the use of the term "Negro" in favor of either "Black," "black," or "Afro-American," many Americans of Mexican descent will not tolerate the term "Chicano" and the militancy it connotes. This ideological and political split is apparent in the absence of bloc voting patterns of the "Spanish surname" community in many parts of the country. (This situation does not apply in Chicano-dominated towns of South Texas, or recently in San Antonio, where the La Raza Unida Party has been very successful in winning local elections).

Pragmatic Organizing Techniques

The divided character of the Mexicano/Mexican American/Hispanic/Chicano communities has made the pragmatic community-organizing tactics of Saul Alinsky particularly effective in the 1960s and 1970s. These same organizing strategies have been central to many working within environmental, consumer, and other kinds of minority movements. Alinsky grew up in the 1930s in Chicago and gained his reputation for mobilizing and politicizing previously apathetic groups. A self-styled "professional radical," he believed firmly in the pragmatic principle that individuals must participate in governing their lives and he spent his life teaching and showing others how to organize. Born in Chicago in 1909, Alinsky went to the University of Chicago, where he later did graduate work in criminology. In the late 1930s, he successfully organized a Black ghetto neighborhood in the Back of the Yards area of Chicago. This was the Woodlawn Organization. In 1940, he established the Industrial Areas Foundation to teach organizers how to mobilize the poor not only in Chicago but also in local communities across the nation.[35] For Alinsky, the minority organizer must always work within definite ideological constraints imposed by (1) the ideas and beliefs of his/her own constituency; (2) the rules, values, and organization of the dominant authority and authorities; (3) the possibility of attracting third parties to the dispute; and (4) the rules and conditions of coverage by the public media or other communication mechanisms in the society.[36]

Alinsky held as a basic rule that the organizer, in dealing with his or her own followers, must never move outside the experience of his or her own constituency. As a first step, this means learning the concerns of one's constituency as intimately as possible. Learning the language, the customs, and the problems of different elements of the constituency is a part of the process. Cesar Chavez, who was trained by Alinsky, developed a variety of organizing techniques to appeal to farmworkers, involving getting farm workers out of jail, helping with driver's licenses and welfare payments, helping to settle immigration problems. The establishment of a credit union was another way of meeting a basic need and also developing an organization.[37]

5. The Minority Politics of the Chicanos

Ernesto Cortez, another Alinsky student who had worked in the United Farm Workers union, began his community organizing effort in San Antonio in 1974 by listening to the complaints of unorganized Mexican American citizens concerned about the annual flooding and lack of drainage in their neighborhoods. This was the beginning of COPS, Communites Organized for Public Service, which since 1974 has managed to have considerable success in redirecting to the central San Antonio area public monies for drainage, street improvement, and parks and has ended the practice of having public monies subsidize Anglo suburban development projects.[38] In Los Angeles, the initial organizing issue that Cortez helped identify to organize the United Neighborhood Organization (UNO) was automobile insurance rates, which were extremely high in East Los Angeles in 1977. By 1979, UNO had developed a community-based Mexican American organization that was able to call a summit meeting with Governor Brown and the executives of ten major insurance firms to secure an agreement from the firms that they would alter their insurance rating system in a way that would lower the rates in East Los Angeles.[39] In each of these cases, the purpose of the organizer was not the issue in and of itself so much as the mobilization of an oppressed Mexican American community. In each case also, obtaining a limited victory for the organization became significant in helping the organization to attract others.

Another aspect of operating within the experience of one's own constituency involves convincing followers that the leader's motives are not selfish. To convince the followers of his or her own commitment, an organizer must be willing to experience personally the danger or hardship or poverty that any followers must face. Martin Luther King, Jr., lived in a situation of everyday danger. In addition, he repeatedly went to jail for his cause. Cesar Chavez lives a Spartan life style and periodically goes on hunger strikes to purify himself and to renew his own and his followers' dedication to the cause. All United Farm Worker staff members must also adopt the life style of the poor and be dedicated to La Causa. Saul Alinsky warns the organizer that his or her own ego must not become involved in the organization. The organizer helps others organize to help themselves and then leaves the situation without taking credit or publicity. This is the pattern of Ernesto Cortez.

The ideological constraints imposed by the rules, values, and organization of the dominant authorities is another extremely important aspect of Alinsky's strategy. Alinsky argued that making the enemy live up to its own rules is one of the most effective tactics. This is essentially an ideological strategy. The legitimacy of the dominant in American society is invariably associated with rules that justify the status of those in authority. These rules may be general ideological notions, such as "all men are equal under law," or they may be very specific rules about building codes or water rates. By identifying and publicizing the fact that the dominant authority is not obeying its own rules, the minority group undermines the legitimacy of that authority. Martin Luther King sought to tell America and the world that while official America preached law and order and equal justice for all, the facts of the situation were quite different. Both King and Chavez insisted on obeying the law or else accepting the penalty for breaking the law. In working with specific issues, knowledge of the "enemy's" rules can be extremely effective. In San Antonio, the COPS group found that often victories are available for the minority if they only know the rules well enough to ask. In obtaining the city's first agreement to fund a drainage project, COPS found the mayor astonished that the project had not been implemented already. The issue was essentially uncontested.[40]

One of Alinsky's basic themes is that a minority group should creatively and imaginatively use the existing rules and values to its own advantage. This means choosing strategies that are legal but that create bargaining situations. The major resource most minority groups can develop is a committed and unified group of people. If a group's target is a bank, Alinsky would have the group members tie up the bank's normal operations by opening and closing bank accounts or by depositing and withdrawing small sums of money. To tie up an airport or other public facility as a bargaining tactic, Alinsky once developed the idea of having a group of people occupy the lavatories for long periods of time. These are tactics that do not violate rules or laws but that advertise the existence of a committed organization and create a bargaining situation. In switching his strategy from farmworker strikes in the fields (which had been rather unsuccessful) to the economic boycott of grapes, Cesar Chavez followed this Alinsky rule. Advocating the boycott of grapes was certainly legal. Furthermore, it was much less of a hardship for Chavez's own followers because it did not ask farm workers to forgo making money as they would have had they gone on strike.

The involvement of third parties as allies in any political struggle is another central strategy for Alinsky-type politics. Often this requires developing multiple issues, as different people are activated by different issues. In practically all community organizational movements in Chicano communities, organizers have sought political support from the Catholic Church or at least relied on the Catholic religion as a unifying force. The Church is an established institution with considerable influence among Mexicanos and Mexican Americans. National political figures, especially if they are running for office, are other favorite third-party allies. Martin Luther King, Jr., attracted the support of John F. Kennedy in 1960. Cesar Chavez and Robert Kennedy attended masses together on several occasions. In the UNO's drive against California insurance practices, the organization attracted the support of Governor Brown, a presidential candidate in 1980.

The tactic of attracting the media to communicate the situation of minorities is integrally related to each of the previous strategies but is especially important for attracting third-party allies. In a sense, the media themselves constitute a third party whose needs and demands must be taken into consideration. To engage the media, organizers may seek to "create" news. Protest marches provide a fairly effective way of attracting media coverage. The March to Sacramento by the United Farm Workers in 1966 and the Poor People's March on Washington in 1968 are examples of this strategy. In 1968, Chicano schoolteachers in Los Angeles led students on a "blowout" to publicize the fact that Americans of Mexican descent had the lowest incomes and the least education of any group in the country. They also pointed out that while Mexican Americans outnumbered Blacks in Los Angeles and in many Texas towns, Chicanos had practically no representation in city, county, state, or national governments. Such marches display the minority group's organization and determination. Other tactics to obtain media coverage include developing and informing contacts in the news media concerning issues important to the cause and providing press releases that are informative and take into consideration the news media's need for drama, human interest, and action.

The Chicano Cultural Movement

The ideological message of the Black Power movement in the United States did not go unheeded by Chicanos in the 1960s and 1970s. The Chicano movement directed much of its attention toward exposing the suppression of Chicano culture and Chicano history by Anglo culture and institutions. History books had to be rewritten. The prevailing image of the Mexican as lazy, as dirty, as a sombrero-clad bandit or other undesirable, had to be opposed in the media and in all public statements. The campaign for bilingual education was a part of this. The 1964 Civil Rights Act required that bilingual education be made available. However, implementing the program throughout the Southwest and in New York has been hindered by the lack of trained personnel.

When bilingual education is not available, the practice has been to put Spanish-speaking children into classes for the mentally retarded. As recently as 1977, a survey of California schools showed that one in every ten had percentages of Hispanics in mentally-retarded classes that exceeded (by 40 percent in some cases) the percentage of Hispanic children in the district.[41]

Emphasizing Mexican art and culture has been a strategy for many Chicano groups who oppose the idea of assimilating in the United States and seek to build a political consciousness that is distinct from and in many ways in opposition to the dominant Anglo culture. In this endeavor, the culture of Mexico as well as Chicano history and practice are the sources of inspiration and reference for Chicanos seeking to use cultural resistance as a basis for the beginning of a social political struggle.[42] Another culture is another frame of reference, another way of seeing the world, another paradigm that when creatively used may lead to new explanations, new creations, and new truths. The purpose is not to make Chicanos in the United States indistinguishable from Mexicans in Mexico. Rather the idea is that Chicanos should develop and use their cultural heritage as a means of escaping the hegemony of United States culture and as a means of being creative in the "progressive development of mass resistance."[43]

United States-Mexican Relations: Chicanos and Immigration in the 1980s

Ideologically, the unique aspect of Chicanos as an interest group in United States politics in the 1980s may lie in the role that Chicanos play in linking the United States and Mexico. Mexico's emergence as a current and potential supplier of oil and natural gas to the United States is coupled with conditions of unemployment in Mexico and a demand for Mexican labor in the United States. The history of the Mexican American throughout the twentieth century has been one structured by the fact that United States businesses have used the Mexican people as a labor pool.

Mexico's own current economic system is geared toward capital-intensive production techniques. The Mexican industrial development plan for 1979–1990 calls for a 10 percent annual industrial growth rate and a 5 percent annual rate of employment growth. Providing jobs is not the first priority for the Mexican government. The plan encourages the production of capital goods, especially those that will produce exportable products. As a second priority the plan attempts to reduce rural-to-urban

5. The Minority Politics of the Chicanos

migration by providing incentives for decentralized industrial-plant location as well as for some labor-intensive methods of production. The priority is growth as a means of providing employment in the long term.

In general, the Mexican economic development plan is not concerned with "solving" the immigration problem. In fact, Mexican officials see immigration as a problem only to the extent that the issue complicates United States-Mexican relations. The migration of Mexican nationals north across the border in search of work has served as a labor escape valve for the Mexican economic development scheme, which at its current state of development and with its emphasis on capital-intensive production cannot provide the employment that is needed domestically.[44] With the end of the bracero program in December 1964, Mexico faced severe problems of urban growth, poverty, unemployment, and underemployment in its border towns. Furthermore, the pressure to provide a labor outlet remained.

The solution was the "twin plants" program that went into effect in June 1966. This program takes advantage of United States tariff codes that allow United States firms to base wholly owned subsidiaries in foreign countries. The United States firm then sends parts to the foreign-based subsidiary for assembly; in turn, these can be returned to the United States for "finishing" and for sale. The United States charges a tariff or duty (between 7 and 15 percent) only on the value added to the assembled parts. This arrangement enables United States firms to take advantage of cheap labor markets in less developed countries. United States firms already had such twin-plant arrangements in Taiwan, South Korea, Hong Kong, Haiti, and Puerto Rico. To implement the program in Mexico, Mexico had to remove its regulations on the operation of United States firms inside of Mexican territory. At first, Mexico created a 20-kilometer "free-trade zone" just inside the Mexican border. In March 1971, the Mexican government abolished this zone and instead opened the nation to such twin-plant operations. Since 1966, many large United States corporations (such as Bendix, Honeywell, Lockheed, RCA, Samsonite, and Zenith) have established manufacturing plants along the border. Although the program requires that United States firms pay 50 percent more than the prevailing minimum Mexican wage, the disparity in wage scales between the two countries makes the operation extremely profitable for United States companies in spite of this requirement. In 1970–1971, the average wage that United States firms had to pay Mexicans was $4.00 for an eight-hour day, about a third of the minimum wage in the United States.[45]

For Mexico, this program has the advantage of providing jobs and provides a flow of United States dollars into the country; these help Mexico's balance of payments. The program, however, creates enormous social problems in the border areas, in addition to attracting more people from the interior of Mexico to the border and eventually to the United States as undocumented workers. The major concern of Mexican policy makers in light of this situation has become one of arguing for the protection of economic and human rights for Mexican citizens in the United States and refusing to adopt any policy that would restrict the movement of Mexican citizens within Mexico.[46]

Still another factor that encourages the northward migration of Mexicans is the fact that businesses based in the United States provide jobs for Mexican laborers. Currently, especially in the Southwest, Mexican immigrants fill many low-paying, low-skill jobs in domestic, gardening, agricultural, factory, restaurant, and hotel situations that United States citizens are unwilling to perform. Private employers in the United States, in general, do not oppose the flow of immigrants as they provide a docile labor force at low wages.

Public Opinion in the United States

Hostile attitudes towards Mexican immigrants have flared at various times in the United States during the twentieth century. Mass roundup deportation campaigns occurred in 1920–1921, 1930–1935, and 1950–1954. In the past, these anti-immigrant episodes have been closely associated with periods of unemployment in the United States. In public-opinion polls, letters to newspapers, and constituents' letters to Congressmen, the dominant opinion about undocumented workers is that Mexican immigrants are a drain on the United States economy. They are perceived as free loaders, demanding expensive social services and bilingual education, and at the same time creating crowded urban conditions that generate crime and social disruption. In spite of studies which support the fact that most undocumented workers in the United States pay federal, state, and local taxes in amounts that exceed the cost of the services they use, the public believes immigrants to be an economic drain rather than a resource.[47]

Opinions vary somewhat according to the area of the country and various interests involved. A *New York Times*/CBS News survey taken in January 1979 reported that 55 percent of the Blacks interviewed believed that undocumented workers take jobs from United States citizens; only 34 percent of the whites interviewed felt this way. The same survey

5. The Minority Politics of the Chicanos

also found a regional difference in the way the public perceives undocumented workers. Of those living in the Northeast, 45 percent believed that illegal immigrants take jobs from United States citizens whereas only 28 percent of those living in the West felt such a situation to exist.[48] The South and the Midwest fell between these ratios. This difference may reflect lack of familiarity with the issue, as most undocumented workers live and work in the Southwest. The survey may also reflect the fact that organized labor is strongest in the East and has traditionally campaigned for more restrictive immigration policies.

The position of Chicano groups with regard to immigration changed rather dramatically in the 1960s and 1970s. In the 1940s and 1950s, groups like the G.I. Forum and the League of United Latin American Citizens favored restrictive immigration policies. Chicano groups in the 1970s, especially those emphasizing cultural pride and heritage, have become active intermediaries for undocumented workers. Chicanos see the rights of immigrants as integrally connected with the welfare of Chicano communities in the United States. Questions involving health care, education, employment, voting strength, and treatment by the police and by the courts are issues that affect Chicanos and immigrants alike. The existence of a pool of undocumented workers who function without individual rights in the United States creates a climate of fear and intimidation that pervades entire Chicano communities. Immigration raids on factories and on residential neighborhoods for the purpose of identifying undocumented workers affect all involved in such factories and barrios, citizen and noncitizen alike.

Still another reason why Chicano leaders seek to emphasize the civil and human rights of immigrants from Mexico, other than basic humanity, is that such a policy is in conformity with the foreign policy of Mexico and enables Chicano leaders to obtain leverage for domestic issues through their linkage with the government of Mexico. In February 1977 and again in September 1979, President José López Portillo of Mexico met with major leaders of Chicano and other Hispanic American organizations, the first meeting in Washington, D.C. and the second in New York, to encourage the group to form an "organized community" that could develop a process of relationships between the government of Mexico and the Hispanic community in the United States.[49]

A final reason for Chicano groups not to favor a restrictive immigration policy involves the political clout that the Chicano political constituency is gaining and will gain as undocumented workers' children, born United States citizens, swell its ranks. In the 1970s, San Antonio, Texas, came to have a Chicano majority, 55 percent of the population in 1979.

Projections predict an even larger majority in the 1980s. The political movement begun by COPS in 1974 has escalated Chicanos into control of the San Antonio city council. In Los Angeles, similar Chicano majorities are forecast for the 1980s, although geographic dispersion and gerrymandering have held the Los Angeles Chicanos far behind those of San Antonio in their political successes. Except for the heavy concentration of Chicanos in East Los Angeles, where gerrymandering has prevented Chicano representation, Spanish-surname individuals are dispersed over a large geographic area (about 5 percent in each census tract).

Although the Chicano movement is extremely young, Chicano leaders since 1968 have demonstrated a creative political skill in developing local community organizations to unify their unorganized constituencies for the purpose of gaining explicit goals in opposition to local elites. Nevertheless, to make any realistic assessment of the Chicano movement's contribution to ideological change in the United States at this time would be premature. Both Blacks and women have made ideological and theoretical contributions. Blacks in their political struggles have made all minority groups aware of the psychic battles that must be waged before any traditional kind of political action is possible. Women have identified the sex-gender structure as an ideological entity that composes a vital part of the political structure.

The history and current treatment of the Mexican and Chicano people as a labor pool for United States businesses makes a Marxist *dependencia* argument very persuasive for many Chicano scholars and leaders.[50] The immigration issue, brought about in part by the huge economic disparities between the United States and Mexico, may well be the focal issue for political attention in the 1980s. Several scholars have proposed that "immigration will be the civil-rights case of the 1980s" for the Chicano people and for Chicano organizations.[51] Whether or how the Chicano movement will be able or willing to use its unique strategic position in politics to open new questions and pose new ideals, possibilities, and perspectives for United States society as a whole remains to be seen.

Notes for Chapter 5

1. This account draws heavily on Carey McWilliams, *North from Mexico* (New York: Greenwood Press, 1968). This classic, originally published in 1948, was one of the very few histories of Mexican American peoples in the Southwest that was in existence in 1968 at the beginning of the Chicano movement.

2. David S. North and Marion F. Houstoun, "A Summary of Recent Data on and Some of the Public Policy Implications of Illegal Immigration," in *Illegal Aliens:*

5. The Minority Politics of the Chicanos

An Assessment of the Issues: A Policy Statement with Background Papers (Washington, D.C.: National Council on Employment Policy, October 1976), pp. 36-51. See also: Robert Lindsey, "U.S. Hispanic Populace Growing Faster Than Any Other Minority," *New York Times*, 18 February 1979, Sec. A, p. 1. A compilation of Spanish-surname population statistics based on the U.S. Census is available in Julius Rivera, "Mexican Americans: The Conflict of Two Cultures," in *The Minority Report: An Introduction to Racial, Ethnic, and Gender Relations*, ed. Anthony Gary Dworhin and Rosaline J. Dworhin (New York: Praeger, 1976), pp. 172-178.

3. McWilliams, p. 66 (note 1 above).

4. McWilliams, pp. 67-71.

5. McWilliams, pp. 84-88.

6. McWilliams, pp. 88-97.

7. McWilliams, pp. 81-84.

8. McWilliams, p. 102. See also Rodolfo Acuña, *Occupied America: A History of Chicanos*, 2nd ed. (New York: Harper, 1981), pp. 3-47.

9. McWilliams, pp. 121-133.

10. McWilliams, p. 137. Acuña, pp. 95-120 (note 8 above). Also Leonard Pitt, *The Decline of the Californios* (Berkeley and Los Angeles: University of California Press, 1966).

11. McWilliams, pp. 162-178.

12. McWilliams, p. 163.

13. McWilliams, pp. 215-216.

14. McWilliams, pp. 167-178.

15. McWilliams, p. 193.

16. For a discussion of this program, see Ernesto Galarza, *Merchants of Labor: The Mexican Bracero Story, An Account of the Managed Migration of Mexican Farmworkers in California, 1942-1960*, preface by Ernest Gruening (Charlotte, California: McNally and Loflin, 1964). See also: Arthur F. Corwin, "Causes of Mexican Emigration to the United States: A Summary View," in *Perspectives in American History*, Charles Warren Center for Studies in American History, Harvard University, 1973, pp. 557-635; hereafter cited as "Causes of Mexican Emigration." Arthur F. Corwin, ed., *Immigrant and Immigrants: Perspectives on Mexican Labor Migration to the United States* (Westport, Conn.: Greenwood Press, 1978).

17. Corwin, "Causes of Mexican Emigration," p. 569 (note 16 above).

18. Corwin, "Causes of Mexican Emigration."

19. Corwin, "Causes of Mexican Emigration."

20. U.S. Congress, House, Committee on the Judiciary, *Illegal Aliens: Analysis and Background*, 95th Congress, 1st Session, report prepared by the Congressional Research Service, Library of Congress (Washington, D.C.: U.S. Government Printing Office, June 1977), pp. 8-9.

21. U.S. Congress, House, p. 4.

22. U.S. Congress, House, pp. 5-8.

23. David S. North and Marion F. Houstoun, *The Characteristics and Role of Illegal Aliens in the U.S. Labor Market: An Exploratory Study*, U.S. Department of Labor (Washington, D.C.: U.S. Government Printing Office, March 1979), p. 39.

24. Corwin, "Causes of Mexican Emigration," p. 586 (note 16 above).

25. For a discussion of Mexican American community political organizations, see Miguel David Tirado, "Mexican-American Community Political Organization, The Key to Chicano Political Power," in *La Causa Política: A Chicano Politics Reader*, ed. F. Chris Garcia (Notre Dame, Ind.: University of Notre Dame Press, 1974), pp. 105-127.

26. Tirado, p. 115.

27. For a detailed account of Cesar Chavez and the United Farmworkers, see John Dunne, *Delano: The Story of the California Grape Strike* (New York: Farrar, Straus, and Giroux, 1967); Peter Mathiessen. *Sal Si Puedes: Cesar Chavez and the New American Revolution* (New York: Random House, 1969).

28. See Tirado, pp. 116-118 (note 25 above).

29. Jose Angel Gutierrez, "La Raza and Revolution" in *Readings on La Raza*, ed. Matt S. Meier and Feliciano Rivera (New York: Hill and Wang, 1974), pp. 231-235. For an account of La Raza Unida Party, see Alberto Juarez, "The Emergence of El Partido de la Raza Unida: California's New Chicano Party," in Garcia, pp. 304-321 (note 25 above). Calvin Trillin, "U.S. Journal: Crystal City, Texas," *New Yorker* (17 April 1971), pp. 102-107. John Shockley, "Crystal City: Los Cinco Mexicanos," in *Chicano: The Beginning of Bronze Power*, ed. Renato Rosaldo, Gustav Seligmann, and Robert A. Calvert (New York: Morrow, 1973).

30. Peter Nabokov, *Tijerina and the Courthouse Raid* (Berkeley, California: Ramparts Press, 1969).

31. Rodolfo "Corky" Gonzalez, "Crusade for Justice," in Meier and Rivera, pp. 243-247 (note 29 above).

32. Chicano Coordinating Council on Higher Education, "MECHA," from "El Plan de Santa Bárbara," in Meier and Rivera, pp. 225-230 (note 29 above).

5. The Minority Politics of the Chicanos 105

33. Frank del Olmo, "Coalition of Hispanic Democrats: Collecting the Votes," *Los Angeles Times,* 16 Dec. 1979, Sec. 4, p. 3.

34. McWilliams, p. 209 (note 1 above).

35. For a discussion of the Woodlawn Organization see Charles Silberman, *Crisis in Black and White* (New York: Random House, 1964).

36. See Saul Alinsky, *Rules for Radicals* (New York: Vintage, 1972). See Michael Lipsky "The Politics of Protest," *American Political Science Review* 62 (March 1968): 1144-1158.

37. John Dunne, *Delano,* pp. 73-75 (note 27 above).

38. Calvin Trillin, "U.S. Journal San Antonio: Some Elements of Power," *New Yorker,* 2 May 1977, pp. 92-100. E. D. Yoes, Jr., "COPS Comes to San Antonio," *The Progressive* (May 1977), pp. 33-36. William K. Stevens, "San Antonio with Mexican Americans in Power, Seen at Crossroad," *New York Times,* 7 April 1979, Sec. 1, p. 1.

39. Joy Horowitz, "UNO's New Leader: Organizing for Power," *Los Angeles Times,* 26 Oct. 1979, Sec. 4, p. 1. "East Side Unit Wins Auto Insurance Plea," *Los Angeles Times,* 31 Jan. 1979, Sec. 2, p. 1.

40. Yoes (note 38 above).

41. "Hispanic Pupils Held Hampered in Tests Tied to English Ability," *New York Times,* 16 Sept. 1979, Sec. 1, p. 66.

42. Juan Gomez Quiñones, *On Culture,* Popular Series #1, UCLA, Los Angeles: Chicano Studies Center Publications, 1977).

43. Quiñones, p. 23.

44. Olga Pellicer de Brody, in "Mexican Immigration: Elements of the Debate in the United States and Mexico," a briefing session sponsored by the International Relations Division, Rockefeller Foundation, Ann L. Craig, rapporteur, Center for United States-Mexican Studies, University of California, San Diego, 10-12 June 1979, pp. 12-18, hereafter cited as "Mexican Immigration."

45. Vernon M. Briggs, Jr., "The Mexico-United States Border: Public Policy and Chicano Economic Welfare," *Studies in Human Resource Development* 2 (Austin, Texas: Center for the Study of Human Resources and Bureau of Business Research, 1974), p. 23.

46. "Mexican Immigration," pp. 10-12 (note 44 above).

47. Wayne A. Cornelius, "America in the 'Era of Limits': The 'Nation of Immigrants' Turns Nativist Again," Working Paper No. 3, Center for United States-Mexican Studies, University of Calfornia, San Diego (June 1979). Prepared for discussion at briefing session "Mexican Immigration," p. 5 (note 44 above).

48. Cornelius.

49. *New York Times*/CBS News National Survey, January, 1979, as cited in Cornelius, p. 6; also William K. Stevens, "Millions of Mexicans View Illegal Entry to U.S. as Door to Opportunity," *New York Times*, 12 Feb. 1979, Sec. 1, p. 1; Sec. 2, p. 10.

50. Acuña (note 8 above). Dependency, *dependencia*, and neo-colonialism are terms, substantially synonyms, referring to a variety of relationships that continue to increase the dependence of less developed nations in Latin America, Africa, and Asia on the industrialized and wealthy nations of the world. See Osvaldo Sunkel, "Big Business and Dependencia: A Latin American View," *Foreign Affairs* 50 (April 1952); Paul Baran, *The Political Economy of Growth* (New York: *Monthly Review Press,* 1957; Modern Reader paperback, 1957); Andre Gunder Frank, *Capitalism and Underdevelopment in Latin America* (New York: Monthly Review Press, 1967; Modern Reader paperback, 1969); Stephen Hymer, "The Multinational Corporation and the Law of Uneven Development" in Jagdish Bhagwati, ed., *Economics and World Order* (New York: Macmillan, 1972).

51. "Mexican Immigration," p. 50 (note 44 above).

Chapter 6

Ideological Change and Minority Politics

This volume has attempted to make two major points about minority politics in relation to ideological change. The first is the relatively well-accepted idea that minority political tactics (even those that include violence) are primarily concerned with symbols and ideology. By definition, minorities are not powerful in the existing political system. They cannot manipulate violence, goods, skills or even symbols in a fashion that is competitive with nation states or global corporations. They have some psychological leverage over the dominant in that they know the dominant in a way that the dominant do not know themselves. This knowledge minorities use either to humor the dominant in hope of reward or to challenge the dominant by articulating and publicizing contradictions in the dominant's self image. When such publicized contradictions are combined with the threat of disruption, they can become an ideological bargaining chip for obtaining specific material and legal benefits. Sometimes these material or legal gains are important symbolically in altering aspects of the dominant ideology.

The second way that minority political tactics can contribute to ideological change is through the ideological appeals minorities use to mobilize their own constituencies. Because the dominant ideology usually defines minorities as inferior in specific ways that confirm the dominant's superior self-definition, minorities are often in a position to be ideologically creative. They operate on the fringes of the dominant code and can often escape the hegemony of its assumptions and values. In struggling to obtain a dignified self-identity, some minorities are strategically able to develop the groundwork for a counter-ideology. To the extent that minorities make statements and arguments that describe the life experiences of the populace, minorities can begin to articulate what more and more members of the society may come to see as reality, especially if the anomalies in the dominant code are glaring.

The Role of Ideology in the Process of Change

The dynamics of ideological, cultural, and social change are not very well understood. Clearly the process is very complex and highly dependent on historical, environmental, economic, and other factors. While the Lockean Liberal position does not address the problem of ideological change or attribute much significance to it, Pragmatic Utilitarian and Marxist approaches offer a variety of explanations.

The Pragmatic View of Ideology and Change

The Pragmatic Utilitarian approach argues that ideas emerge from the experiences people have as they live in the world and communicate with one another. The task of government is to devise procedures to enable all these experiences to be articulated and to permit the formulation and execution of policies that will provide the greatest pleasure for the greatest number. Ideas emanate from experience and in turn are processed into public policy. Using this approach, it is possible to look at the history of American political procedures to evaluate how they have performed this function.

First in this evaluation is the political party system of the United States. Pragmatic Utilitarians argue that the electoral system has managed to incorporate the ideas of minorities that could not be suppressed into one of the two national political parties during presidential elections and/or has allowed these minority interests to dominate the regional area. In this way, presidential elections, particularly the critical elections of 1828, 1896, and 1932, served to integrate minority interests such as those represented by the western states in 1828, the Populists in 1896, and labor and urban ethnic groups in 1932 into electoral participation.[1]

On the state and local levels, political machines, often controlled by immigrant minorities such as the Italians or the Irish, fought their way into political recognition through state caucuses, conventions, and a general control of local patronage systems. The electoral process and the political party system of the United States, while certainly not perfect, have operated to introduce Pragmatic Utilitarian ideas into a predominantly Lockean Liberal political system.

The infusion of new ideas was most clearly demonstrated in the 1932 election and the subsequent New Deal policies that became possible primarily because of the collapse of the "free market" economy in 1929. The ideas for this change had been articulated and considered in a variety of ways prior to 1932. Taking this kind of approach, Pragmatic Utilitarians argue that minorities hammmered out and introduced innovative ideas that provided an alternative ideology. This new ideology gave minorities more voice in governmental decisions, legitimized the redistribution of wealth to minorities, and provided a different justification for government activity.

The court system is another procedural area where the Pragmatic Utilitarian can demonstrate that the ideas of minority groups, especially Blacks, have altered the dominant coding of the society. While admittedly slow and cumbersome in its operations, the process of judicial review has allowed minorities to challenge the dominant coding of the society and in some instances to effect a change.

Critiques of the Pragmatic Utilitarian View

The Pragmatic view of how minorities can change the dominant ideology of the society has many critics. While political parties in the United States are not entirely dead, a number of developments suggest that the political parties are less able to reflect the views of minorities than they were prior to 1950. The growth of global corporations and the increased use of the mass media are primarily responsible for this situation. The effectiveness of television as a propaganda device has made the party system more responsive to money and less responsive to grassroots organization. Global corporations have resources to spend on campaign contributions and advertising that overwhelm the resources of any other set of institutions in the society.

The second problem is the failure of the Pragmatic Utilitarian ideology to deal with the ability of power to corrupt and the ability of government agencies to be unfair. An examination of many of the New Deal programs, especially the redistributive ones, shows that while many programs generally benefit the poor at least to some extent, they provided a more significant long-term opportunity for economic concentration in the hands of a few. The gains for minorities—specifically for Blacks—were often mainly symbolic. The same argument can be made for the civil-rights movement of the 1950s and 1960s. While enormous symbolic gains were made—legal bans on segregation, attainment of voting rights, and consciousness raising in the nation—economic advances have in fact been few and far between for most Black people in America.

The Marxist View of Ideology and Change

Most Marxists argue that ideological change reflects economic change. Ideologies are a part of the superstructure that interacts with the economic conditions of production in a dialectical process. The problem of how and whether ideas and ideology that emanate from material conditions can assume an independent role in history, at least temporarily, has been a subject of considerable debate among Marxists. Marx and Engels in *The Communist Manifesto* suggest a materialist interpretation when they argue that the means of production determines the relations of production in every epoch. The ruling class of each epoch derives its material and intellectual power from its control over the dominant means of production. The ruling ideas of a society are those of the ruling class. At the same time, Marx calls upon the proletariat to develop its own class consciousness as it pursues its conflicts with the ruling class in the class struggle.

In other works, such as the *Eighteenth Brumaire of Louis Bonaparte*, Marx gives weight to the notion that while ideas emanate from material conditions, at some crucial points in history ideas can temporarily direct the course of events. The controversy surrounding this issue has not been resolved. While Marx believed that the ruling class would use its ideology to suppress and subjugate the lower classes, he also believed that through political struggle, organization, and the help of some intellectuals, the proletariat could break away from the dominant coding of the ruling class to develop a "true" proletarian class consciousness. This new class consciousness was critical to the Marxian revolution.

A variety of Marxist scholars and political leaders have offered different explanations for how the class consciousness of the proletariat can develop. Lenin argued that the consciousness of the proletariat had to be introduced from outside the proletariat, that it would not spontaneously develop from within. Stalin, as is well known, used force, terror, and indoctrination to institute and maintain "a new ideology" in Soviet society. Mao, in China, emphasized compulsory participation in Marxist ideological thought.

Many western Marxists, upon viewing the Russian and Chinese experiences, have become rather pessimistic about the possibility of seizing the means of production and having a true socialist society develop. Unless fundamental ideas and interrelationships change along with the political and economic changes, old patterns of domination persist. Some, such as Louis Althusser, have gone so far as to advocate that the class struggle must take place *within* theory.[2] Still others like Georg Lukács argue that the ideological crisis of the proletariat in developing class consciousness

". . . must be solved before a practical solution to the world's economic crisis can be found."[3]

Lukács distinguishes between objective economic totality, objective class consciousness, and the subjective real thoughts and feelings that people have about their lives. What people subjectively feel and think is a "false consciousness." This false consciousness is extremely important, however, as it may promote and realize "the objective aims of society of which it is ignorant and which it did not choose." The consciousness of the proletariat is divided within itself. The immediate concrete interests of the proletariat exist in a dialectical relationship with the objective impact of these interests as they relate to the society as a whole. The false consciousness of the proletariat must be examined as an aspect of historical totality and as a stage in the historical process. In bourgeois society, the bourgeois and the proletariat are the only "pure classes" as they are ". . . the only classes whose existence and development are entirely dependent on the course taken by the modern evolution of production . . . ."[4] The proletariat in developing hegemony to effect a revolution will have to organize all of society in accordance with its interests. Its capacity to do this will hinge on the extent to which it can become conscious of the actions it must take to organize power.

While Lukács's concept of totality draws heavily on German idealism, his emphasis on the priority of ideological change to effect economic change is particularly insightful. Also, his idea that the subjective consciousness of the proletariat and their political actions have unintended consequences that advance objective class interests is one that opens new possibilities.

In looking for evidence of subjective proletarian class consciousness, western Marxists tend to find more hope when examining European societies than they do in studying the situation in the United States. Among people living in the United States, class consciousness in the sense of subjective awareness of class is very weak. Many Marxists in the United States find themselves describing and documenting the intellectual, cultural, and economic hegemony of the bourgeois rather than finding evidence of growing proletarian class consciousness.

The Linguistic or Semiotic Model of Change

The linguistic or semiotic model is one that draws an analogy between language and ideology according to basic assumptions drawn from Ferdinand de Saussure's linguistic analysis.[5] This model argues that a language or set of concepts understood by members of a society must be distinguished from the act of speaking. While individual speech acts are what compose a language, the language itself has a life and a structure separate from any particular act of speaking or any one individual. By analogy, ideology as a semiotic system would be equivalent to a language and political interaction equivalent to speech.

While economic conditions may well influence language and ideology, the linguistic model suggests that both language and ideology have a structure and an internal dynamics of their own. Furthermore, ideology, like language, becomes embedded in the unconscious of individuals, where it becomes an organizing principle for interpreting the world and for individual self-identity. Social analysts drawing on the linguistic model have sought to identify and explore symbolic opposites as well as symbolic continuities in the cultural life of societies for the purpose of understanding more fully the phenomena of ideological structure.[6] Most of the studies using this approach tend to be static in that they seek to document patterns of continuity rather than explain the dynamics of change. They are significant to this discussion of ideological change because they show that ideology is not a completely dependent variable but has a structure and a life of its own. Moreover, they connect ideological systems and symbols to the psychological identities of people in the society as well as to the interrelationships people have with one another.

A major attraction of the linguistic model as applied to ideology is the suggestion it offers that (within the constraints provided by economic, social, and ideological forces) human beings as individuals and as groups can change the ideology of the society through their political interactions in the same way that speakers can change a language as they use speech acts to relate to one another. The process is not linear or direct, but it does play a role in shaping ideological, social, political, and ultimately economic change.

The semiotic model would expect ideological change to occur according to the dialectical relationship between the structure of the dominant code(s) and the human interactions that occur in the society, just as language and speech interact dialectically. Semiotic systems are composed of signs organized as binary oppositions. While all social and cultural phenomena are signs that are defined by networks of interrelationships, of particular interest are the psychic identities of individuals as superiors and inferiors expressed in the dominant coding(s). Minorities serve as "an other" to the dominant values. They represent what the dominant are not. For this reason, when minorities in their political activities begin to challenge their status in society, they challenge the dominant ideological codings and disrupt accompanying established patterns of interaction. Their political activities change dispositions and generate new levels of subjective consciousness. These effects influence the ideological structure of the society and ultimately the economic and political structure as well.

The Role of Theoretical Activity

To expect that any one minority group will emerge with a theory that can become a viable dominant ideology is not realistic. While the political activities of minority groups can change dispositions, raise consciousness, and set the groundwork for a new theoretical statement, they are unlikely to articulate a well-developed theory. Clearly, some groups will contribute more than others, as will some minority-group leaders. Others in the society also can contribute to changing the disposition of people in a society. An artist, a singer, a poet, a commentator, a social critic, or a writer may articulate a direction for a new approach that captures the reality of many people's lives. Ideological events in the nation's history, such as the Vietnam war or Nixon's Watergate crisis, may serve as catalysts for this process. All of these interactions provide the ideological material with which the theorist must work to develop an explanation or theory that can capture the truth of everyday life as most people in the society experience it. Such a theory might well articulate a new ideology. A moral quest exists in this process, for it is not a predetermined one. Choices that have consequences must be made. An ideology is morally unacceptable if it does not seek to narrow the economic and political gap between the rich and the poor in the world or if it offers the individual no variety of choice in determining how to participate in the shaping or building of a better political order.

Specific Ideological Contributions of Minority Politics

While it is perhaps premature to assess accurately the ideological contributions of minority politics in establishing new ideological assumptions or reconfirming old ones in slightly different ways, some general conclusions do emerge from an examination of the politics of three of the largest and most strategically placed minorities in United States politics. One of the most poignant contributions of Black politics in the United States has been the delineation and exploration of the psychological dimensions of self-identity and its relationship to the dominant ideology as well as to the power structure. Leaders such as

W. E. B. Dubois, Marcus Garvey, and Malcolm X were pioneers in this area.

The struggle by Blacks against the Lockean Liberal ideology which is able to define and treat human beings as property is another extremely important ideological contribution. Ever since the founding of the National Association for the Advancement of Colored People at the beginning of the century, the Black movement in the United States has insisted on the ideological priority of the principle of equal treatment under the law. Innumerable battles have been fought, and some won, attempting to make the dominant in the United States live by this principle of both Lockean and Pragmatic Utilitarian ideology. The court battles as well as the entire nonviolent civil-rights movement under Martin Luther King, Jr., James Farmer, A. Philip Randolph, Huey Newton, and countless others have made significant changes in the public consciousness and have gained limited, symbolically important goals that emphasize the ideal of political and legal equality for all citizens.

One direct result of the Black movement has been the psychological awakening and political training of women in American society. Women identified with the plight of Blacks and were able to use the insights gained from the Black movement to begin to put together their own kind of minority politics. Perhaps the most important ideological contribution of the women's movement is its identification and description of the sex-gender system of "patriarchy" as it has operated in history and as it currently operates in the United States. To describe the patriarchy calls attention to the theoretically ignored reproduction function in society and delineates the way sex roles are unconsciously organized in modern society as well as in history. By demonstrating that the sex-gender organization of society has been kept in the private sphere and not allowed to be a part of public policy debate, women have brought to consciousness the fact that the patriarchy functions to keep women in a status of being psychological, economic, political, and social minorities. Since the patriarchy dominates what Lockean Liberals and Pragmatic Utilitarians regard as the private sphere, the major ideological thrust of the women's movement is to make the sex-gender system public business and to destroy the idea that the public and the private can be separated politically.

The Radical Feminists have been the pioneers in developing the idea of a sex-gender system that is separate from the economic system. Radical Feminists have drawn special attention to the many unconscious practices, traditions, and symbols that keep women psychologically, economically, and politically oppressed. The Socialist Feminists build on the Radical Feminists' work to argue that the sex-gender system exists in a dialectical relationship with the economic relations of society. It is not surprising that the capitalist model of production does not consider the bearing, rearing, and nurturing of children to be work. Yet, argue the Socialist Feminists, women and the work that they do are what support the capitalist organization of production and work. If women were to receive a fair wage for the reproductive work and nurturing that they do, the capitalist system would not be able to survive. The Socialist Feminists reason that since capitalism is dependent on the patriarchal sex-gender system, a change in the sex-gender system should have an impact on the economic system. Both Radical and Socialist Feminists continue to document the innumerable ways in which the patriarchy as a sex-gender system penetrates all aspects of society, including the organization of space, housing, language, work, and especially psychological orientation. Since all these elements of society involve power relationships, Radical and Socialist Feminists believe they all should be considered a part of the public sphere, open for public debate.

To argue that the public and the private cannot be distinguished is to make a major break with the Lockean Liberal and the Pragmatic Utilitarian ideologies. It expands the definition of what is political to practically all aspects of living. This perception is perhaps one of the potentially most revolutionary ideological insights developed by any currently active minority group. The Lockean Liberal position holds that the government, or the public, should be concerned with allowing people to preserve themselves by protecting their right to acquire property. The Pragmatic Utilitarian has a broader view of the public sphere as concerning actions which have consequences for others. In many respects the Radical and Socialist Feminist positions on this issue garner legitimacy from the Pragmatic Utilitarian position, although the two are quite different. The Pragmatic Utilitarian would argue that the exact line where the public and the private spheres separate from one another is always open for debate. The Radical and Socialist Feminists argue that to maintain that there is such a line is an ideological fiction that tends to oppress women. While the Radical Feminists are concerned primarily with ideological activity, the Socialist Feminists argue that as the ideological assumptions change concerning the public and the private issue, as well as on other matters, social and economic change will follow. Socialist Feminists note that as the women's movement has progressed, women have entered the work force in large numbers. This trend generates both social and economic changes in childrearing patterns, unemployment levels, family and marital relationships, socialization into sex roles, concern about equal pay for equal work, and a variety of other issues. For Socialist Feminists, the agenda is to work simultaneously on ideological and economic issues as they relate to the sex-gender system.

The Chicano movement in the United States is ideologically interesting because it brings into immediate domestic focus many of the issues that arise out of the United States government's and the global corporations' relationships with the less-developed countries in the world. The issue of labor is central. Mexico has a surplus of unskilled labor, a rapidly growing population, and a shortage of capital. The United States and United States corporations have capital, technology, and a demand for cheap, unskilled labor. Immigration policy becomes the focal point for this disequilibrium because it divides Lockean Liberals from Pragmatic Utilitarians and in addition presents Pragmatic Utilitarians with severe internal dilemmas.

The Lockean position gives priority to the United States demand for unskilled cheap labor. Accordingly, immigration policy should allow Mexican citizens to come to work in the United States with a minimum cost to the United States in terms of social services. Thus programs such as the Bracero Program (1942–1964), whereby Mexican men contracted to work for no more than 18 months at a time in the United States and then return home, are ideal. Faced with the situation of large numbers of undocumented Mexican migrants coming into the United States, the Lockean priority is to allow economic interests to be satisfied. (President Reagan, for example, agreed in June 1981 to start a pilot program of 50,000 guest workers from Mexico.)

The Pragmatic Utilitarian position is faced with a dilemma on this issue. Allowing the flow of undocumented Mexican workers into the United States generates serious violations of basic civil-rights priorities. Because these undocumented workers fear being sent back to Mexico, they become a group of people without civil rights. Employers are in a position not only to pay extremely low wages (thereby depressing domestic wages), but they can also cheat, abuse, and sometimes even physically torture undocumented workers without any interference from legal authorities. While employers argue that they cannot persuade domestic workers to take the available jobs that guest workers fill, critics of temporary-worker programs argue that employers prefer undocumented workers because they are more docile and can easily be controlled with threats of raids from the Immigration and Naturalization Service (INS).

Pragmatic Utilitarian policy makers, including labor unions and civil-rights groups, advocate giving amnesty to those workers currently in the United States, tightening border surveillance, and having no new programs for temporary workers. This policy was the essence of Jimmy

6. Ideological Change and Minority Politics

Carter's somewhat confused program on immigration. Ronald Reagan's policy also advocated amnesty for those who have lived in the United States ten years and more intense border surveillance to keep out new immigrants. However, the Reagan Administration also wants to have a temporary work program, to penalize employers who hire undocumented workers, and to deny access to federal courts for individuals seeking to appeal the rulings of the Immigration and Naturalization Service.

All three of these latter measures are repugnant to those who place a high priority on the Bill of Rights. The temporary work program creates a group of people in the United States whose civil rights are not protected. To be able to penalize employers who hire undocumented workers, everyone would have to carry some kind of identification card, a practice that smacks of South Africa's apartheid and other fascist regimes. The purpose of denying access to the federal courts for appeals would be to make it easier to send undocumented workers back to Mexico. Not only would this denial be unfair to temporary workers, but it would also jeopardize entire communities of United States citizens of Mexican heritage. In the past, when the Immigration and Naturalization Service deported large numbers of people to Mexico, many United States citizens were included in the roundups.

The international aspect of the immigration problem further complicates the ideological issues, especially for those of Pragmatic Utilitarian persuasion concerned about the consequences of political acts. Should the political community be considered only the United States, or is not the well-being of the United States closely tied to the well-being of the global community, especially that of bordering nations? Mexico, in the midst of a development program, needs a safety valve for its burgeoning population growth. As a wealthy, industrialized nation of immigrants, how can the United States close the border to impoverished immigrants from neighboring Mexico? To argue that the United States should severely limit or close its doors to immigrants from the developing nations is very close to the idea that the only course for the United States is one of becoming nationally stronger and richer, regardless of the state of the rest of the world. (This has been called the "lifeboat policy," advocated by Garrett Hardin.[7]) Many labor-union and civil-rights groups find themselves in an ideological dilemma on this issue.

The community organizing efforts of the Chicano movement are another significant contribution of Chicano politics. Black organizations have tended to use the charisma of particular leaders who outline a new identity for Black people to keep their own constituencies together (Marcus Garvey or Malcolm X), or have rallied around cultural, religious, and organizational aspects of the Black Christian church (Martin

Luther King, Jr.). The pragmatic community-organizing tactics of Saul Alinsky have been most successfully used by a variety of local Chicano organizations in ways that are quite original. While these tactics are not particularly ideologically interesting in and of themselves, the process they employ is germane ideologically. The strategy is to begin with issues that are central to their own people and then move to other issues once an organizational structure has been established. Often the initial issues are not ideological at all but relate to a specific grievance or a particular inconvenience. In many ways, this is a revival of the old political-machine tactics of urban United States in the late nineteenth and early twentieth centuries. Certainly this kind of political activity can have an important impact on local politics. Many groups with unorganized constituencies—such as the deaf, the handicapped, consumer groups and environmental groups—look to the Chicano movement for examples of successful organizing tactics.

An Assessment of the Semiotic Model as Applied to Ideologies and Minorities

The semiotic model contributes a fundamental insight that distinguishes it from other models which tend to draw analogies from natural-science disciplines that study and explain the behavior of inanimate phenomena. This insight is the recognition that networks of relations among people have symbolic meanings as signs and as semiotic systems. The ideological constructs and the important relations among people in a society are inseparable, for each defines the other in a dialectical way. The structure of the ideological or semiotic system imposes conditions and constraints on human interactions. In turn, human interactions are what give meaning to ideological systems. Individual human interactions are not symbolic in and of themselves but are the constituent elements that compose collective ideological systems. The networks of human interactions have primacy in this relationship, for unlike natural-science phenomena symbolic systems or ideologies have few intrinsic properties as independent entities.

A second important contribution of the semiotic model lies in its implications for policy making. It suggests that symbolic or ideological systems develop historically as a part of a culture and cannot be easily or quickly changed. They persist as a language persists. Hence past revolutions may need to be regarded as relatively superficial rather than as total social, economic, ideological, and political changes. A corollary of this proposition is that the dynamics of ideological change depend on a multitude of human interactions in a society. Imposing an alien ideological system by force on a society certainly alters human interactions. However, the semiotic model suggests that such ideological change will be incomplete. Fundamental ideological changes must develop from within the society as individuals alter their interactions in response to an ideal or in response to conditions in the environment or society.

In comparison with Lukács, the linguistic or semiotic model does not identify an objective totality; neither does it designate a particular class whose consciousness and activities are crucial to achieving that totality. Instead, the linguistic model suggests that ideologies are semiotic systems which are structured by means of oppositions. Minorities represent an opposition value in a dominant coding, a sign that explains or confirms the dominant values which the minority is not. When minorities refuse to accept the identity or coding of being inferior, they can upset not only established patterns of interaction but also the structure of oppositions within the dominant ideological system. This rupture makes lasting ideological, economic, political, and social change possible.

Notes for Chapter 6

1. William Nisbet Chambers, "Party Development and the American Mainstream," in *The American Party Systems: Stages of Political Development*, eds. William Nisbet Chambers and Walter Dean Burnham (New York: Oxford University Press, 1967), pp. 3–32.

2. Louis Althusser and Etienne Balibar, *Reading Capital*, 2nd ed. (New York: Pantheon, 1971). Louis Althusser, *For Marx* (New York: Pantheon, 1970). For a secondary source that reviews Althusser's ideas, see Alex Callinicos, *Althusser's Marxism* (London: Pluto Press, 1976).

3. Georg Lukács, *History and Class Consciousness: Studies in Marxist Dialectics*, trans. Rodney Livingstone (Cambridge, Mass.: MIT Press, 1968, 1971).

4. Lukács, p. 79. For a discussion of class consciousness, see pp. 46–82.

5. Ferdinand de Saussure, *Course in General Linguistics* (New York: McGraw-Hill, 1966) *(Cours de linguistique générale*, first published Paris 1916). For an excellent introduction to some of the ideas that have developed from this model, see *Structuralism*, ed. David Robey (Oxford: Oxford University Press, 1973).

6. See for example, Claude Lévi-Strauss, *The Savage Mind* (Chicago: University of Chicago Press, 1969). Michel Foucault, *Madness and Civilization: A History of Insanity in the Age of Reason* (New York: Vintage, 1973).

7. Garrett Hardin, "Living on a Lifeboat," *Bioscience* 24 (October 1974): 561–568.

Index

Abortion, 67, 72, 74, 80, 81
Abzug, Bella, 71
Acuña, Rodolfo, 87, 101, 103, 106
Africa
 Black emigration to, 25, 27, 31
 Black Panthers and, 53
 in Black politics, 21
 independence movements, 55
 Universal Negro Improvement Association in, 55
African Freedom movements, 46
Afro-American Movements, 47
Afro-American Student Organizations, 53, 54
Afro-American Studies, 53–54
Agitation, in Black protest, 25
Agriculture, Chicanos in, 88–90
Alabama National Guard, 42, 44
Albany, GA, 39, 42
Ali, Muhammad, 55
Alianza de Pueblos Libres, La, 91
Alienation, of minorities, 12, 19
Alinsky, Saul, 91, 94–97, 105, 118
Allen, Robert, 46, 61
Alston v. School Board of Norfolk, 36, 60
Althusser, Louis, 110, 119
American Colonization Society, 27
American Federation of Labor, racial discrimination, 37–38
American Indians, 25, 51
American Negro Labor Congress, 38
Angola, 55
Anthony, Susan B., 66

Antifeminist arguments, 72–73
Antifeminist positions, in women's politics, 69
Apartheid, 55, 117
Arab nations, 55
Arafat, Yasser, 56
Arizona, Mexican settlement, of, 85–87
Armed rebellion, risk for Blacks, 25, 26
Art, Radical Feminist outlook on, 76
Asia, Black Panthers and, 53
Association, freedom of, 5
Assumptions
 ideological, 1–2
 negative power and, 14
"Atlanta Exposition Address, The," Washington, 28, 35
Authority
 legitimation of, 1
 source in Lockean theory, 4
Automobile insurance rates, 95, 97
Aztecs, in Hispanic culture, 93
Aztlán culture, 93

"Back to Africa," 31
Bakke case, 53
Baldwin, James, 43
Balibar, Etienne, 110, 119
Baran, Paul, 102, 106
Bayes, Jane H., 3, 5
Bennett, Lerone, 27, 42, 58, 60
Bilingual education, 97–98, 100
Birmingham, AL, 39–42, 44
Birth control, 67, 72–74

Index

"Black," breaking out and, 15
Black Caucus, Congressional, 57
"Black is beautiful," Garvey, 29
Black-liberation schools, 53
Black movement
  churches in, 117
  women's movement and, 65, 67, 114
Black Muslims, 21-22, 31-34
  business activities, 32
  foreign linkages, 56
  separatist program, 31-34
Black Panther, The, 48, 53, 62
Black Panthers, 22, 46, 48-53
  Black Studies and, 53-55, 62
  PLO linkage, 55-56
Black people
  consciousness raising for, 28, 52
  cultural nationalism, 54-55
  distribution, 86, 87
  migration to the North, 28, 37
  separatist movements, 15, 26-28, 31-34
  strategic position, 25-26
  in union movement, 37-38
  World War I and, 28
Black politics, 25-63
  Chicano contribution to, 102
  Garvey view of, 29-30
  ideological assessment of, 56-58
  ideological contributions, 113-114
  international linkages in, 21-22, 55-56
Black Power movement, 45-47
  Chicano parallel, 97-98
Black pride
  Black Muslims and, 32-33
  Dubois and, 32
  Garvey and, 28, 29, 32
Black Star Line, 31
Black Student Unions, 54
Black Studies movement, 53-55
Black-white coalitions, 47-48
Bourdieu, Pierre, *facing* 1
Boycotts, 19
  of grapes, 96
  women in, 66
Bracero program, 89, 99, 116
Bracey, John H., Jr., 27, 58, 59
Breakfast program, of the Black Panthers, 53
Breaking out
  of invisibility, 20

  language in, 15
  minority tactics, 13, 14-16
  negative power vs., 15
  tactical constraints on, 22
Breitman, George, 32, 46, 59, 61
Briggs, Vernon M., 99, 105
Brisbane, Robert, 52, 54, 56, 62
Broderick, Francis L., 27-28, 59
Brody, Olga Pellicer de, 99, 102, 105, 106
Brotherhood of Sleeping Car Porters, 37
Brown, Edmund G., Jr., 95, 97
Brown v. *Board of Education*, 36
Buchanan v. *Warley*, 36, 60
Bunch, Charlotte, 74, 83

California
  Chicano organizations in, 91
  Mexican settlement, of, 85-88
Californios, 88
Callinicos, Alex, 110, 119
Cambridge, MD, 42, 44
Canada, Black emigration to, 25
Capitalism
  in the Markist position, 6
  patriarchy and, 80
  women's unpaid labor in, 80, 114-115
Carmichael, Stokely, 45-48, 50, 61
Carribbean area, Universal Negro Improvement Association in, 55
Carter, Jimmy, 56
Catholic Church, Chicanos and, 96-97
Censoring, 19
Census Bureau, 58, 62
Central America, Black emigration to, 27
Chambers, William Nisbet, 108, 119
Chavez, Cesar, 91, 94-96, 104
Chicago
  Alinsky in, 94
  1968 riots, 52
"Chicano"
  breaking out and, 15
  objection to term, 93
Chicano Coordinating Council, 91, 104
Chicano cultural movement, 97, 98
Chicano movement
  ideological change and, 116-118
  international linkages, 22
Chicanos
  distribution of, 85-86

history in the U.S., 87–89
immigration policies affecting, 88–89, 99–101
in labor force, 85–90, 98–101, 116
minority politics of, 85–106
organizing techniques, 94–97
political clout, 101–102
political organization, 90–92
public opinion on, 100–102
strategic position, 92–94
See also Hispanics; Mexican Americans
Child care, 80
Children, extrauterine, 74
China, 110
"Cholo," 92
Christianity, Black Muslims and, 30, 33
CIO. *See* Congress of Industrial Organizations
Civil disobedience, 16
by Blacks, 42–43
moral responsibility in, 40–42
Civil Rights Acts
of *1875*, 27
of *1964*, 44, 50, 67
of *1965*, 44, 45, 50
of *1967*, 97
Civil-rights movement, 57
international linkages, 21–22
women in, 66–67
Civil War
Black separatism and, 27
in women's history, 66
Clark, Mark, 52
Class in the U.S., 7–8
Class consciousness, 110–111
Class struggle, in Marxist position, 7
Cleaver, Eldridge, 48, 51, 61
Cleveland, OH, Black politics in, 57
Cloward, Richard A., 18, 21, 23, 37, 43, 44, 57, 60–62
Colorado, Chicanos in, 86, 88
"Colored," 32
Columbia University, 53–54
Communist Party/Parties
in Black union movement, 37–38
Dubois in, 28
women in, 66
Communities Organized for Public Service (COPS), 95, 96, 101
Community control of police, 53

Community Services Organization (CSO), 91
Confrontation, in Black politics, 43
Congress, Black Caucus in, 57
Congress of Industrial Organizations (CIO), 38
women in, 66
Congress of Racial Equality, 38, 39, 42, 44, 45
on Black Power, 47
Consciousness raising, 19, 111
Black 28, 52
women's, 68
"Conservative," meaning of, 4
Constituencies
for nonviolent action, 40
protest appeals to, 17
Constraints, on majority strategy, 22
Contraception, 72–74
arguments against, 72
oral, 67
CORE. *See* Congress of Racial Equality
Cornelius, Wayne A., 100, 101, 105, 106
Cortez, Ernesto, 95
Corwin, Arthur F., 89, 90, 103, 104
Courts
in Black strategy, 25, 36–37
Black successes in the, 36–37
minority influence in the, 109
"Creative tension," in nonviolent action, 41
Cronon, E. David, 29, 59
Cruzada para la Justicia, La, 91
Crystal City, TX, 91
Cubans/Cuban Americans, 86, 92, 93
Cuffe, Paul, 27, 58
Cultural movement, Chicano, 97–98
Cultural nationalism, Black, 54–55
Culture, Radical Feminist outlook on, 75–76

Deacons for Defense and Justice, 46, 49
de Beauvoir, Simone, 73, 83
Deckard, Barbara Sinclair, 66–68, 82, 83
Delano, CA, 91
Delany, Martin R., 27
del Olmo, Frank, 92, 104
Democratic National Conventions, 47, 52
Democratic Party, Hispanic caucus in, 92
Demystification activities, 19

Index

Dependencia/dependency, 102, 106
Dependencies
 creating, 13, 16–20, 22
 minority use of, 13, 16–20
Desegregation
 Black protest for, 25
 of education, 36
Developing countries, Black interest in, 56
Dewey, John, 5, 9
Dinerstein, Dorothy, 75, 83
Dining-car equality, 36
Direct nonviolent mass action, 38–39
Domestic labor, 77
 unpaid, 80, 114–115
Dominant, the
 dependence on subordinate, 16
 ideologies, of, 1–2
 minority leverage over, 107, 109
 negative power and, 13–14
 women in, 65
Douglas, Mary, 13, 23
Douglass, Frederick, 27
Dubois, W. E. B., 27–28, 55, 59, 114
 integrationist strategy, 35–37
Dunne, John, 91, 94, 104, 105

East Los Angeles, CA, Chicanos in, 95, 101, 102
"East Side Unit," 95, 105
Eavesdropping, on minorities, 19
Economic independence, antifeminist arguments against, 72
Economics
 Radical Feminist outlook on, 76
 Socialist Feminist position, 76–77
Edelman, Murray, 8, 9
Education, 25
 antifeminist arguments against, 72
 bilingual, 97–98, 100
 desegregation of, 36
 of minorities, 19
Edwards, Adolph, 29, 59
Eisenstein, Zillah R., 76, 80, 83, 87
Elementary and Secondary Education Act, 57
Elkins, Stanley, 13, 23
Ellison, Ralph, 14, 20, 23
Emancipation Proclamation, 27
Emigration, in Black politics, 25–27
Enfranchisement, Black protest for, 25

Engels, Friedrich, 76, 83, 110
Equal Employment Opportunity Commission, 67
Equal Pay Act, 67
Equal Rights Amendment (ERA), 67, 70
 Socialist Feminist views on, 81
Equality, Black protest for, 25
Essien-Udom, E. U., 32, 59
Ethics, minority challenges of, 19
Ethiopia, 30, 55
Ethnic groups, political influence, 108

False consciousness, 111
Family
 nuclear, 79–80
 Radical Feminist attack on, 75
Fanon, Frantz, 15, 23
Fard, W. D., 31, 33
Farmer, James, 38, 39, 114
Farming, Chicanos in, 88–90
Femininity, Radical Feminist outlook on, 75
Firestone, Shulamith, 73–75, 83
Flexner, Eleanor, 66, 82
Foner, Philip, 52, 61
Ford, Gerald, 92
Ford, Nick Aron, 53, 62
Foreign policy, Black interest in, 55–56
Foreman, Ann, 76, 80–81, 83, 84
Forman, James, 39
Forten, James, 27, 58
Foucault, Michel, 12, 23, 112, 119
Frank, Andre Gunder, 102, 106
Franklin, John Hope, 27, 31, 58, 59
Free African Societies, 27
Freedoms, in traditional ideologies, 5, 8
Freedom Rides, 39, 42
 women in, 66
Freud, Sigmund, 72–73, 78, 79, 83
Friedan, Betty, 67

G.I. Forum, 90–91, 101
Galarza, Ernesto, 89, 103
Gamson, William A., 41, 60
Gandhi, M. K., 21
Garvey, Amy Jacques, 29, 31, 59
Garvey, Marcus, 28–31, 55, 59, 114, 117
Garvey movement, 21, 28–31
 business aspects, 30–31
 King on, 45
 religion and, 30

Gary, IN, Black politics in, 57
Gender questions, Radical Feminist perspective, 74-76
  Socialist Feminist outlook, 77-81
  in women's politics, 68-69
Global corporations
  less developed countries and, 116
  political influence, 109
God, Garvey view, 30
Goffman, Erving, 12, 14, 23
Gompers, Samuel, 37
Gonzales, Rodolfo "Corky," 91, 104
Government
  in the Lockean outlook, 4
  in the Marxist outlook, 7
  in the Pragmatic Utilitarian outlook, 5-6
Government agencies, unfairness, 109
Grandfather clauses, 36
Greensboro, NC, 39
Group interests, in traditional ideologies, 22
Guadalupe Hidalgo, Treaty of, 88, 91
Guilt, in minority self, 12
Guinn v. *U.S.*, 36, 60
Gupte, Pranay B., 58, 62
Gutierrez, Jose Angel, 91, 104
Guyana, 56

Haiti, Black emigration to, 27
Haley, Alex, 32, 59
Hamilton, Charles, 47
Hampton, Fred, 52
Happ, Howard, 72, 83
Hardin, Garrett, 117
Hare, Nathan, 53, 54, 62
Hartz, Louis, 3, 9
Hayes, Rutherford B., 27
Health clinics, Black Panther, 53
Henderson v. *U.S.*, 36, 60
Hilliard, David, 52
"Hispanic," 93
Hispanic American, definition of, 93
Hispanic American Democrats (HAD), 92
Hispanic Lawyers Association, 92
"Hispanic Pupils," 98, 105
History, Radical Feminist outlook on, 76
Horowitz, Joy, 71, 83, 95, 105
House Committee on Internal Security, 52, 61
House Committee on the Judiciary, 89, 104

Houston, Sam, 87
Houstoun, Marion F., 87, 102, 104
Hughes, Langston, 38
Hymer, Stephen, 102, 106

Ideological change
  contribution of minority politics to, 113
  economic change and, 111
  linguistic-semiotic model of, 111-113
  minorities and, 8-9, 113
  minority politics and, 107-119
Ideological frameworks, of minority politics, 3-9
Ideology/Ideologies, 1 *et passim*
  challenges of, 2, 3
  ideal types, 1
  language and, 112
  in minority politics, 107
  role in change, 107-113
  traditional, 7-8
  in the unconscious, 112
Illegal immigrants, 87-90, 117
Immigration and Naturalization Service (INS), 89, 101, 116-117
Incentives, for political action, 17-18
Incest taboos, 79
India, 55
  in Black politics, 21
  nonviolence in, 40
Information gathering, 40
Innovation, minority politics and, 20
Institute for Defense Analysis, 54
Insurance rates, 95, 97
Integrationist ideologies, in Black politics, 26
Integrationist movements, in Black politics, 34-44
Interest groups
  in Marxist position, 7
  in politics, 1
  in Pragmatic Utilitarian outlook, 6
International linkages, in minority politics, 21-22
International political situation, minority-group strategy and, 21-22
Interstate Commerce Commission, 39
Invisibility of minorities, 19
Islamic nations, 55

Jackson, George, 52

Index

Jackson, Jesse, 56
Jackson, Jimmie Lee, 44
Jagger, Alison M., 72, 83
Japanese Americans, 51
Jersey City, NJ, Black rioting in, 44
Job discrimination, persistence of, 57
Jobs, for women in World War II, 66
Johnson, Lyndon B., 44, 47
Jonestown suicides, 56
Juarez, Alberto, 91, 104
Jury service, 36

Karenga, Ron, 55, 62
Kennedy, John F., 42-44, 97
Kennedy, Robert, 43, 97
King, Martin Luther, Jr., 39-43, 45-46, 50, 55, 60-61, 95-97, 114, 117-118
Kinship systems, 78-79
Kluger, Richard, 36, 60
Ku Klux Klan, 27

Labor, political influence, 108-109
Labor force
  Chicanos in, 85-90, 98-101, 116
  women in, 66, 115-116
Lacan, Jacques, 78, 84
Language
  breaking out and, 15
  ideology and, 112
  Radical Feminist outlook on, 76
Lasswell, Harold, 8, 9
Latin America
  Black Panthers and, 53
  Universal Negro Improvement Association in, 55
"Latino," 93
Leaders, in breaking out tactics, 15
League of Struggle for Negro Rights, 38
League of United Latin American Citizens (LULAC), 90, 101
Legal actions, in Black strategy, 36-37
Legal Defense and Education Fund, of NAACP, 36
Legitimacy, in minority politics, 22
Legitimation of authority, 1
Lenin, V. I., 110
Lesbianism, 74-75
"Letter from Birmingham Jail," 40-41
Lévi-Strauss, Claude, 112, 119
  in Socialist Feminist outlook, 78-80

"Liberal," meaning of, 4
Liberal tradition, 2-3
Liberia, in Garvey movement, 31
Libya, Black Muslims and, 56
"Lifeboat policy," 117
Lincoln, C. Eric, 31, 59
Lindsey, Robert, 87, 102
Linguistic model of change, 111-113, 118-119
Lipsky, Michael, 17-18, 23, 40, 60, 94, 105
Little, Malcolm. See X, Malcolm
Liuzzo, Viola, 44
Locke, John, 4, 9
Lockean Liberal framework, 4-5
Lockean Liberal position, inadequacy of, 7-8
Lockean Liberals
  and the Black ideological struggle, 114
  Black politics and, 56-58
  essential outlook, 4
  ideological change and, 108-118
Lomax, Louis, 36-39, 60
López Portillo, José, 101
Los Angeles, CA, Chicanos in, 95, 97, 101-102
Louisiana, 46, 49
Love, Radical Feminist outlook on, 75
Lowery, Joseph, 56
Lowndes County Freedom Organization, 46, 47-48
Luckács, Georg, 110-111, 119
Lynch, Hollis R., 31, 59

McComb, MS, 39
McGuire, George, 30
McKissick, Floyd, 45, 50
McWilliams, Carey, 85, 87, 88, 94, 102, 103, 105
Madness, "other" status, 12
Mao Zedong, 110
Marches, 38, 40, 44, 47, 97
Marketplace equality, Black demand for, 25
Marriage, Radical Feminist outlook on, 75
Martyrdom, in Black protest, 25
Marx, Karl, 77, 110
Marxism, Dubois and, 28
  Socialist Feminist attitudes on, 80
Marxist position, 6-7
  Chicanos and, 93

dependency theory, 102
  ideological change and, 110–111
  inadequacy of, 7–8
Mass action, direct nonviolent, 38–39
Mass demonstrations, 16
Mayors, Black, 56
Media
  Black Panthers and, 50–51
  in organizing, 97
  nonviolence and, 40
  in politics, 109
  protest appeals, to, 17
Mentally retarded classes, Hispanic pupils, in, 98
Meredith, James, 45, 47
Mexican Americans
  definition of, 93
  See also Chicanos; Hispanics
Mexican American Legal Defense Fund (MALDEF), 91
Mexican American Political Association (MAPA), 91
Mexican American Women's National Association, 92
Mexican American Youth Organization (MAYO), 91
Mexican War, 87–88
Mexico
  Chicanos and, 85, 87, 89–90, 98–100, 116–118
  culture of, 98
  oil and gas resources, 98
  U.S. relations with, 98–100
Meyer, August, 27, 28, 58, 59
Militancy, legal successes and, 36
Mill, John Stuart, 5, 9
Mills, C. Wright, 6, 9
Minorities, 1 *et passim*
Minority, defined, 11
Minority politics, 1 *et passim*
  ideological change and, 107–119
  ideological contributions to, 111–118
  significance of, 11–23
Mississippi, 45
Mississippi Freedom Democratic Party, 47
Mitchell, Juliet, 78–80, 84
Model Cities Program, 57
Money, in Lockean outlook, 4–5
Monroe, NC, 49
Montgomery, AL, 38–39, 44

Montgomery Improvement Association, 38
Moore, Cecil, 42
Moore v. Dempsey, 36, 60
Moorish Science Temple, 31
Motherhood, Radical Feminist outlook on, 75
Movimiento Estudiantil Chicano de Aztlán (MECHA), 91, 104
Muhammad, Elijah, 31
Muhammad ibn-Abdullah, the Prophet, 33
Muhammad Speaks, 32
Mulford, Don, 51
Murray, George, 54
Music, Radical Feminist outlook on, 76

NAACP. *See* National Association for the Advancement of Colored People
NAACP Legal Defense Fund, 36
Nabokov, Peter, 91, 104
Nashville, TN, 39
Nation of Islam. *See* Black Muslims
National Association for the Advancement of Colored People (NAACP), 35–39, 91
  founding of, 28
  ideological change and, 114
  voter registration drive, 44
National Council of La Raza, 92
National Farm Workers Association, 91
National Organization for Women (NOW), 67, 70, 71
National Rifle Association, 49
National Urban League, 37
National Women's Political Caucus, 71
Nature, antifeminist arguments based on, 72
Negative power
  breaking out vs., 15
  in minority tactics, 13–14
Negotiation, nonviolence and, 40–41
"Negro," 32, 93
Negro Factories Corporation, 31
Negro/negro preference, 28
Negro World, 30
Neo-Marxism, 54–55
Neo-Marxist ideologies
  in Black politics, 26, 53
  Radical Feminist attitude, 75–76
New Deal
  minority influence in, 109

Index

women and, 69
New Left organizations, women's issues and, 68
New Mexico, Mexican settlement of, 85–88
New Right, women's politics and, 71
New York City, Black rioting in, 44
New York Times/CBS News National Survey, 100–101, 106
Newark, NJ, Black politics in, 57
Newton, Huey, 46, 48, 49, 51–53, 55, 62, 114
Niagara Movement, 28, 35
Nigeria, 55
Nineteenth Amendment, 66, 70, 81
Nixon, Richard M., 92, 113
Nixon administration, Blacks and, 57
Nonviolence, 38–39
  campaign steps, 40–42
  loss of appeal, 49–50
  theory of, 39–44
Nonviolent mass action, direct, 38–39
North
  Black migration to the, 28
  escape to the, 25
North, David S., 87, 90, 102, 104
NOW. *See* National Organization for Women

Oedipal concept, 78–79
Olson, Mancur, 17, 23
Organization of African Unity, 46
Organization for Afro-American Unity, 33, 46
Organizing tactics, Chicano, 94–97, 118
Organizing techniques, law-enforcing, 95–96
"Other"
  Blacks as, 28
  mad/insane as, 12
  Mexican Americans as, 92
  minorities as, 112
  in subordinate/superordinate relationship, 11
  women as, 73–74

"Pachucos," 92, 93
Palestine Liberation Organization (PLO), Black Panthers and, 55, 56
Pan African Conferences, 21–22, 28
Pan African Congresses, 55

Pan African movement, Garvey, 29
Parks, Rosa, 38
Paterson, NJ, rioting in, 44
Patriarchy, 73, 114
  Socialist Feminist outlook on, 76–81
  in socialist countries, 79
Peace and Freedom Party, 52
Philadelphia, PA
  Black protests in, 42
  rioting in, 44
Pitt, Leonard, 88, 103
Piven, Frances Fox, 18, 21, 23, 37, 43, 44, 57, 60–62
Plessy v. Ferguson, 36
"Pocho," 92
Police, Black Panthers and, 48–53
Police brutality, 50–53
Police patrols, of Black Panthers, 48–51
Political Association of Spanish Speaking Organizations (PASSO), 91
Political change, minorities and, 2
Political machines, 118
  minority influence in, 108
Political parties
  decline of, 109
  minority influence in, 108–109
Political rights, antifeminist arguments against, 72
Politics, 1 *et passim*
Poor People's March on Washington (1968), 97
Populists, as a minority political influence, 108
Poststructuralism, Socialist Feminist position on, 78–80
Power, capacity to corrupt, 109
Powerless, politics of the, 1, 11
Pragmatic Feminists
  on biological differences, 74
  position in women's politics, 69–71
  Socialist Feminists compared with, 76–77, 81–82
  strategies for, 70–71
Pragmatic Utilitarians
  and the Black ideological struggle, 114
  Black politics and, 56–58
  essential outlook, 4
  framework, 5–6
  ideological change and, 108–118
  inadequacy of, 7–8

Preferences, for Blacks, 56
Primary elections, voting in, 36
Prisoners, women as, in society, 72
Prisons
　Black organization in, 52
　minority population in, 58
"Proceedings of the Woman's Rights Conventions," 70, 83
Proletariat, 6–7
Propaganda, 19
Property
　in the Lockean outlook, 4
　in the Pragmatic Utilitarian outlook, 5
　in the Socialist Feminist outlook, 76–77
Protests, 16, 19
　appeals targets, 17–18
　Black forms of, 25, 44, 46
　in Chicano organizing, 97
　the dominant's responses to, 18–19
　tactics against, 21
Psychoanalysis, 78
Public/private distinction
　in Socialist Feminist outlook, 80
　in women's politics, 69, 74, 114–115
Public relations techniques, 19
Puerto Ricans, 92, 93
　in the Census, 86

Quiñones, Juan Gomez, 98, 105
Quotas, for Blacks, 56

Rackley, Alex, 52
Radical Feminists, 73–74, 114–115
　in women's politics, 79
　Socialist Feminists compared with, 76–77, 81–82
　strategies of, 74–76
Randolph, A. Philip, 37–38, 114
Raza Unida Party, La, 91, 94
Reagan, Ronald, Chicanos and, 116, 117
Reconstruction era, 27
Reiter, Rayna R., 78, 84
Religion
　antifeminist arguments based on, 72
　in breaking out tactics, 15
　of Blacks, 30. *See also* Black Muslims
　Garvey movement and, 30
Repression, forms of, 18–19
Repressive reactions, to minority politics, 26

Reproductive processes, women's disadvantages, 73–74
Resources, Lockean view of, 4
Reverse discrimination, 53
Richardson, Gloria, 42
Right to Life movement, 71
Rioting, as Black protest, 25, 44, 46
Rivera, Julius, 87, 103
Romantic love, Radical Feminist outlook on, 75
Roosevelt, Franklin D., 38
Rubin, Gayle, 78, 79, 83, 84
Rudwick, Elliott, 27, 28, 31, 58, 59
Russia, 110

Sacramento, CA, march to, 97
San Antonio, TX, 91, 94–96, 101–102
San Francisco State College, 54
San Quentin Prison, 52
Santa Fe, NM, 85
Saussure, Ferdinand de, 111–112, 119
Schlesinger, Arthur, Jr., 43, 61
School equality, 36
　Black demand, 25
SCLC. *See* Southern Christian Leadership Conference
Seale, Bobby, 46, 48, 51, 52
Segregation, 36
　of Blacks, 27
　reduction in, 57–58
Self-defense organizations, Black, 46–53
Self-hatred, in minorities, 12
Self-identity
　Black Muslims and, 31–32
　in ideological change, 113–114
Self-purification, nonviolence and, 40–42
Selma, AL, 44
Semiotic model of change, 111–113, 118–119
Seneca Falls, NY, Woman's Rights convention *(1848)*, 70
Separatist movements, 15
　breaking out tactics and, 15
　Black Muslims, 31–34
　in Black politics, 15, 26–28
　Dubois and, 28
　Garvey, 28–31
　Radical Feminist, 74–76
Separatist politics, 19
Serve the People Program, 52

Sex-gender system
　feminist outlooks on, 76–81
　ideological change and, 114–115
　Radical Feminist perspective, 74–76
　Socialist Feminist outlook, 78–81
　women's politics and, 69–70
Sharecropper Union, 38
Shockley, John, 91, 104
Sierra Leone, Black emigration to, 27
Silberman, Charles, 94, 105
Sit-ins, 39
　women in, 66
Slave revolts, 25
Smith v. *Allwright*, 36, 60
SNCC. *See* Student Nonviolent Coordinating Committee
Social disruption, in minority-group tactics, 21
Social Security, women's rights in, 67
Socialist Feminists, 114–115
　positions in women's politics, 69, 76–81
　Pragmatic Feminists compared with, 76–77, 81–82
　Radical Feminists compared with, 76–77, 81–82
　strategies for, 81–82
Socialist Party, women in, 66
Society, women as prisoners in, 73
Sociobiology, antifeminist arguments based on, 73
Soledad Brothers, 62
Sorensen, Theodore, 43, 61
South Africa, 55, 117
South America, Black emigration to, 25
Southern Christian Leadership Conference (SCLC), 38–40, 42, 45, 55, 56
"Spanish surname," 86, 94
　Census and, 86
Speech, freedom of, 5
Spying, on minorities, 19
Stalin, J. V., 110
Stanton, Elizabeth Cady, 66
State, in Marxist outlook, 7
Statistical Abstract of the United States, 58, 62
Steinem, Gloria, 71
Stevens, William K., 95, 101, 105, 106
Stigma
　minority as, 11–12
　minority politics and, 18

　negative power and, 14
Strategic positions
　of Blacks, 25–26
　of minority groups, 20–22
Strikes, 19
Structuralism, Socialist Feminist outlook on, 78–80
Struhl, Paula A. Rothenburg, 72, 83
Student Nonviolent Coordinating Committee (SNCC), 38–39, 42, 44–45
　Black studies and, 53
　in Vietnam protests, 47
　women in, 67
　women's issues and, 68
Students for a Democratic Society, 51, 67
　Black studies and, 53
　women's issues in, 68
Subordinate, the
　challenges of, 14–16
　dominant's dependency on, 16
　insights of, 14
　negative power as, 13–14
　position of, 11–13
Suffering Party, 30
Sunkel, Osvaldo, 102, 106
Supreme Court, Black politics and, 27, 36
Symbols, in minority politics, 18–19, 107

"Talented Tenth," 35
Television in politics, 109
Territorial separation, Black movements for, 26, 32
Terror tactics, 16, 19
Texas
　Chicano organizations in, 91
　Mexican settlement of, 85–88
Theoretical activity, in minority politics, 113
Third parties
　nonviolence and, 40–41
　protest appeals to, 17–18
　in Malcolm X strategy, 34
Third World, in Malcolm X strategy, 34
Tirado, Miguel David, 90, 91, 104
Tijerina, Reies López, 91
Trade Union Unity League, 38
Trade unions, women in, 80
Traditional ideologies, inadequacy, 7–8
"Trickle down theory," 8
Trillin, Calvin, 91, 95, 104, 105

Tuskegee Institute, 29, 35
Twin plants programs, 99

Unconscious, the
 ideology in, 112
 patriarchy and, 78–79
"Underclass," 57
Undocumented immigrants, 89–90, 117
Unemployment, Black/white, 58
Union movement, Black workers and, 37–38
United Farm Workers, 91, 95, 97
United Mexican American Students (UMAS), 91
United Nations, 56
United Neighborhood Organizations (UNO), 95, 97
United States, nonviolence in, 40
Universal Negro Improvement Association, 28–31, 55
Universities, Chicano movement and, 91

Veterans Administration, 90
Vietnam War, 55, 113
 Black Panthers and, 51
 protests against, 47
Violence, breaking out and, 15
Voter mobilization, 16
Voter registration
 in Black politics, 34
 drives for, 43–44
Voting, in primary elections, 36

Wallace, George, 44
War on Poverty, 57
Washington, Booker T., 27–28, 30, 59
 Garvey and, 29
 integrationist strategy, 34–35
Washington, DC
 march on (1933), 38
 march on (1963), 44
 Poor People's March on (1968), 97

Watergate affair, 113
Watson case, 53
Weathermen, 51
West Indies, Black emigration to, 25
"Wetbacks," 89
White, Theodore, 43, 61
Williams, Robert, 49
Woman's Rights Convention, Seneca Falls (1848), 69–70
Women
 Blacks compared with, 65, 67
 in dominant institutions, 65
 exchange of, 78–79
 minority politics of, 65–84
 negative-power use, 13
 suffrage, 66
Women, USA, 71
Women's Bureau, Labor Department, 66, 82
Women's movement
 Blacks and, 65, 67, 114
 history of, 66–69
 international linkages, 22
Women's politics
 Chicano contribution to, 102
 diluting issues, 66
 Lockean Liberal ideas in, 68–69
 Pragmatic Utilitarian ideas in, 66–69
Woodhull, Victoria, 74
Woodlawn Organization, 94
World War I, Blacks and, 28
World War II, women during, 67

X, Malcolm, 32–34, 43, 47, 49, 55, 59, 114, 117

Yale University, 54
Yoes, E. D., Jr., 95, 96, 105
Yorty, Sam, 92
Young, Andrew, 56

Zimbabwe, 55
"Zoot suiters," 92, 93